KU-567-283

Secondary School Examinations

'the helpful servants, not the dominating master'

Jo Mortimore and Peter Mortimore;
revised and up-dated by Clyde Chitty

Bedford Way Papers 18
Institute of Education, University of London
distributed by Turnaround Distribution Ltd

CITY OF BIRMINGHAM
LIBRARY
POLYTECHNIC

CITY OF BIRMINGHAM
POLYTECHNIC LIBRARY

BOOK
No.   06096182

SUBJECT
No. 373.1262 Mor

First published in 1984 by the Institute of Education, University of London,
20 Bedford Way, London WC1H 0AL. Second edition 1986.

Distributed by Turnaround Distribution Ltd, 27 Horsell Road,
London N5 1XL (telephone 01-609 7836)

The opinions expressed in these papers are those of the authors and do not necessarily reflect those of the publisher.

© Institute of Education, University of London, 1984, 1986
All rights reserved.

ISBN 0   85473   259   4 second edition
(ISBN 0   85473   167   9 first edition)

British Library Cataloguing in Publication Data
Mortimore, Jo
   Secondary school examinations : 'the helpful servants, not the dominating master'. —
   2nd ed. — (Bedford Way Papers, ISSN 0261-0078;18)
   1. Examinations — England   2. Education, Secondary — England
   I. Title   II. Mortimore, Peter   III. Chitty, Clyde   IV. University of London,
   Institute of Education   V. Series
   373.12'62'0942   LB3056.G7

ISBN 0-85473-259-4

Printed in Great Britain by Reprographic Services
Institute of Education, University of London.
BWP18—35/37/147/I1-001-088-0886-JR

Contents

Acknowledgements

This paper is based partly on a report by Jo Mortimore, funded by the National Evaluation of the EEC/DES Transition to Work Project directed by Professor Alan Little. Thanks are due to Tessa Blackstone, Tricia Broadfoot, Derrick Byford, Alan Hornsey, Jon Lauglo, Martin McLean, Desmond Nuttall, Malcolm Skilbeck and Carol Varlaam for helpful comments. In addition, we should like to thank Keith Weller of the Schools Council for allowing us access to unpublished material; and Pat Wood and Owen John for word-processing.

J.M.   P.M.

I should like to thank Denis Baylis, Denis Lawton, Jo Mortimore and Peter Mortimore for their help and advice with the preparation of this revised edition.

C.C.

Jo Mortimore was a Research Officer at the University of London Institute of Education between 1977 and 1980, first attached to the Thomas Coram Research Unit and later to the Department of Economic, Administrative and Policy Studies in Education. With Tessa Blackstone, she is author of *Disadvantage and Education* (Heinemann Educational, 1982).

Peter Mortimore is Director of Research and Statistics of the Inner London Education Authority. He completed his Master's degree at the London Institute of Education and is a co-author of *Fifteen Thousand Hours* (Open Books, 1979).

Clyde Chitty has taught in London comprehensive schools and at a community college in Leicestershire. He now works in the Post-Sixteen Education Centre at the University of London Institute of Education and as a tutor in the Curriculum Studies Department. He is reviews editor of the journal *Forum* and a member of the editorial board of *Socialism and Education*.

Preface to the 1984 Edition

This paper documents a number of issues concerned with secondary school examinations in England and Wales. It begins by describing the evolution of the present system over the last one hundred and fifty years, and traces growing unease over the constraining effects of examinations. The pressures for reform and the various proposals for changes in examinations are discussed and evidence of the resistance to change, particularly from the universities, is presented.

The methods of assessment adopted in Sweden, France and the USA are reviewed briefly in order to see what lessons might be learnt from other systems. Some of the techniques used in these countries are gaining support in Britain, with the growth of pupil profiles and graded assessments. The pressing need for change is emphasized by the current recession and its effect on unemployment. In addition, the interest in alternative forms of assessment of many within the education system — coupled with the setting up of the new Secondary Examinations Council, chaired by Sir Wilfred Cockcroft — suggests to us that the time is ripe for a thorough reappraisal of the system of public examinations. We believe that the innovations in assessment should be encouraged and built upon in order to develop more positive means of assessing pupils' learning.

Preface to the 1986 Edition

Any new or revised paper on examinations and assessment cannot claim to be anything more than an interim statement. As with so many other aspects of the current educational scene, we are dealing with an area of rapid change and innovation. This new edition of an important paper originally published in 1984 attempts to evaluate some of the main developments that have taken place in the past two years, while accepting that it leaves a lot of questions still unanswered and is by no means intended to be the final word on the subject.

* * *

Table 3 on page 30 was originally prepared by Martin Grant for the year 1980 for Janie Whyld (editor), *Sexism in the Secondary Curriculum* (Harper and Row, 1983) and updated by Kate Myers for the year 1982 for an article in *Comprehensive Education,* No. 49, Summer 1985, pp.14-17.

1   Development of the Examination System

The externally-validated examinations used in schools today have developed out of the formal tests introduced in the nineteenth century by the universities and some of the professions. In order to understand fully the evolution of school examinations it may be helpful briefly to review the development of these earlier forms of assessment.

When social roles and status were ascribed principally by birth or patronage, there was no need for examinations. But during the early nineteenth century several factors contributed to the need for formal assessment of those aspiring to enter university, the professions or the Civil Service.

By the beginning of the last century the traditionally conservative Universities of Oxford and Cambridge abolished their religious admission tests and adopted a more utilitarian approach. They began to take their responsibilities for assessment, both at the beginning and at the end of degree courses, more seriously and to introduce more searching examinations for degrees. With the passing of the Oxford Examination Statute in 1800, written examinations were accepted as a means of identifying the ability and rewarding the attainment of students (Lawson and Silver, 1973, p.257).

At about the same time, members of the established professions were beginning to realize that they could enhance their status and increase their power by restricting entry to those who could demonstrate they had achieved certain levels of competence. The first professional qualifying examinations were introduced in 1815 by the Society of Apothecaries. In 1835 written examinations were introduced for solicitors.

The expansion of the public service at home and abroad also highlighted the inadequacy of recruitment by patronage. The Northcote-Trevelyan reforms of the Civil Service led to the introduction in the 1850s of competitive entrance examinations. Military and naval academies at Sandhurst and Woolwich quickly followed suit. By the middle of the last century, therefore, assessment by written competitive examination was increasingly common at what we would now term the post-school level, providing 'gateways' to the universities, the professions and to the civil and military services.

This development affected, in turn, the schools attended by potential applicants. Responding to pressure from parents, many of the grammar schools began to prepare pupils specifically for these entrance examinations; some even had a special 'Civil Service Class'. Grammar schools flourished, for there was no shortage of pupils aspiring to fill the burgeoning clerical and administrative posts associated with an industrial, exporting nation with a far-flung empire.

In the main these developments affected only the education of boys. The education of girls was restricted generally to those from the upper and middle classes who were taught at home by governesses. A few girls attended private schools where they were taught to read and write and to follow some domestic studies. The more socially distinguished schools taught what they considered young ladies needed in order to appear accomplished and attractive in the matrimonial market. (For example, music, drawing, embroidery, French.) Little serious attempt was made to develop girls' intellects. Consequently there was little need for girls to be involved in competitive public examinations.*

The expansion of both examinations and grammar schools led to the realization of the need for a method of assessing the quality of education provided, and for some evidence of the standards being attained. In order to meet this need a system of 'Locals' developed. This was an independently-commissioned evaluation of a school by a respected outsider, usually a fellow of an Oxford or Cambridge college, or a local clergyman. Locals were, however, an expensive and a somewhat haphazard practice, and many schools, including those most needing inspection, chose not to invite external assessment.

In 1857 the 'Exeter Experiment' was set up, whereby, with the co-operation of Exeter University, competitive examinations were organized for pupils from local schools. This was rather different to the 'Locals' system for the focus was on the achievement of individual pupils rather than on the efficiency of the school. When attempts were made to emulate Exeter and to co-ordinate the system, the universities were seen as the

---

* The Taunton Commission of 1868 noted a general indifference to girls' education. There were, however, rare instances of enlightened and far sighted innovations by individuals or groups, for example the Governesses Benevolent Institution which, in 1848, founded Queen's College in London. From this college emerged the impressive female educationalists, Dorothea Beale (later principal of Cheltenham Ladies' College) and Frances Buss (later principal of the North London Collegiate School for Girls).

obvious source of expertise. Accordingly, in 1858, both Oxford and Cambridge introduced a new form of 'Locals' for the examination of pupils and, from 1877, issued certificates. 'The age of school examinations controlled by university boards had begun' (Lawton, 1980, p.88). The emphasis had, however, veered from the external assessment of the school to the external assessment of individual pupils. Gradually other universities also established procedures for examining school pupils. London University, for example, developed a School Leaving Certificate to satisfy the needs of schools for a statement of pupils' academic achievement, and Matriculation examinations to set standards for university entrance.

Non-university examining bodies, such as the Royal Society of Arts, the City and Guilds of London Institute and the College of Preceptors, also organized examinations as did some professional bodies although, as Lawton has documented, there was pressure on them to use the existing Matriculation examinations where possible.

As a consequence of all these developments there was, by the end of the last century, a patchy and uncoordinated array of examinations. Severe curricular demands on the grammar schools to meet the needs of the various examining bodies brought pressure for uniformity, but little consensus emerged on who should be responsible for school examinations.

Both the Taunton Commission (1868) and the Bryce Commission (1895) had recommended that a central body be created to be responsible for examinations, but little was done to implement these suggestions. By the beginning of this century, although the creation of the Board of Education (1899) and of local authorities (1902) made available a co-ordinated school system in which to locate examinations, opposition to central control was widespread among teachers and local authorities. Moreover, the Board of Education was not keen to assume direct control, preferring to wield influence indirectly. It appears that there was insufficient public confidence in teachers to allow them control of a national system of examinations. (The College of Preceptors had failed, in 1903, to gain recognition for their examinations from the Board of Education.) But the higher-status universities, which had continued to increase their control at the expense of some of the professional associations, were viewed favourably by opponents of centralization — in particular by the local authorities.

Eventually, in 1917, a compromise was reached with the formation of the Secondary Schools Examinations Council (SSEC). This consisted of twenty-one representatives, six from local authorities, five from teacher ranks, and ten from the universities. Although the proportion of university representatives has varied at different times (and was removed completely for a time in 1946), their influence remained and was extended through the university examination boards which had overall responsibility for the setting and marking of examinations.

In 1911 the Consultative Committee of the Board of Education had reviewed examinations and discussed both the advantages and disadvantages of formal written papers. The Committee concluded in favour of examinations as being 'not only necessary but desirable in secondary schools' (Consultative Committee on Examinations in Secondary Schools, 1911). However, the Committee urged that a re-organized inspectorate work closely with the examining bodies. It was their hope that the results of school inspections would be taken into account by the examiners and, conversely, that the examiners' findings would also be made available to the inspectorate. This co-operation, it was considered, would 'afford a test both of the general excellence of the schools' work and of the attainment of individual pupils'. However, this suggestion for what can be seen as an early form of public accountability of schools was short-lived.

Soon after their formation the SSEC produced, in 1917, plans for the co-ordination of new School Certificate and Higher School Certificate examinations.

School Certificate and Higher School Certificate
The two new examinations were to be administered by the university examinations boards. Broadfoot argues that acknowledging the universities as the appropriate bodies to conduct secondary school examinations encouraged the emphasis on intellectual and academic attainments at the expense of aesthetic, practical and non-cognitive aspects of education.

> It is hardly surprising that the traditional pinnacles of the education system which had for long been the almost exclusive monopoly of the élite should be given the task of determining the structure of the newly emerging mechanisms of social selection. Nor is it surprising that they were determined in that élite's own interests (Broadfoot, 1979, p.34).

The School Certificate examination for sixteen-year-old grammar school pupils was seen as an assessment of the school rather than the pupils. It was meant to control the curriculum of the secondary school and to encourage schools to provide a good and balanced education. Candidates were expected to pass in five subjects, including one from each of three groups (humanities; languages; mathematics and sciences). Art, music and practical subjects were considered inferior and were relegated to a fourth group from which only one subject could be offered. Since the School Certificate assessed the school, and since entire classes were entered for it, pupils who found the examinations too difficult were, nonetheless, expected to enter. The whole-class condition was removed in 1929.

The subject-group requirements were a source of persistent criticism. For example, members of the Association of Headmistresses considered that their female pupils were penalized by the need for a pass in mathematics or science. From 1938 the rules were relaxed in order to allow candidates to offer either a language or mathematics/science.

The Higher School Certificate was a test not of the school but of eighteen-year-olds after a further two years' study. Candidates specialized in two main and two subsidiary subjects. (The former, separate university entrance examination, or Matriculation, was incorporated within the new certificates.)

Thus, over a period of about a century, a system of public, external examinations for academically-inclined pupils developed. This system became a form of 'quality-control'. Its aims were to increase competition and to select and reward merit. The long association between the examination system and the universities underpinned the academic emphasis of most school examinations and ensured their applicability for the more academically able students.

The 'non-academic' strand

What was provided for the rest of the school population during these years? What sort of education was given to 'the hewers of wood and the drawers of water', and how was it assessed? What preparation was made for the majority of young people to participate in the life of a leading industrialized nation?

The limited elementary education for the mass of the population was provided mainly, before 1870, by private religious or philanthropic efforts. The narrow curriculum consisted of the three Rs, supplemented perhaps by some accounts for boys and domestic studies for girls. But the prime purpose of schooling for the poorer classes was to instil moral discipline and social subordination — not aims which called for written, external assessment.

The years from 1830 to 1870 witnessed increasing concern over the educational provision for the general population, partly out of concern over our better-educated foreign competitors and partly out of fear of social unrest. In 1833 the first Parliamentary grants for education were distributed through the National and British Societies. The creation, in 1839, of the Committee of the Privy Council on Education greatly increased the authority of the state in education. Gradually, the state and voluntary bodies collaborated in providing a system of elementary education explicitly for the poor.

The payment of government grants to elementary schools was refined in the Newcastle Commission's Revised Code of 1861. The Code empowered school inspectors to test the efficiency of pupils' learning in order to assess the amount of grant to be paid directly to the school managers. The implementation of the Code resulted in an emphasis on the rote learning of the three Rs and in widespread oral testing of schoolchildren by teachers. It was hoped that, by frequent rehearsal, pupils would be able to meet the demands of the inspectors so that the school would receive its grant intact — and the teachers their salaries. Judge comments that examinations of this kind 'appealed to the nineteenth-century sense of frugality and effectiveness' and reflected a concern that public funds would be spent more judiciously if the results were tested and success in raising standards rewarded (Judge, 1974).

These examinations were very different from the examinations which were developing in the grammar schools at this time. They were oral rather than written, with no question of external validation or resulting qualification. 'Passing' the tests did not equip pupils with any formal recognition of attainment. The tests only assessed pupils in so far as pupils' achievements were the yardstick for assessing the financial worth of the teacher. On leaving elementary school most people received no more education and, therefore, did not take formal examinations.

There were, meanwhile, developments outside statutory schooling which led to the creation of examinations in technical and practical subjects. The 'self-education' movement, mediated through the Mechanics' Institutes, encouraged working people to attend evening classes related to their trade. Government concern over industrial decline, exacerbated by inadequate (or non-existent) technical education at home and improved education abroad, led to the establishment of the City and Guilds of London Institute in 1878 and of the London Polytechnic in 1883. The City and Guilds aimed to administer a system of examinations which would 'provide apprentices and others with goals at which to aim' (*City and Guilds Broadsheet,* 1978). After the Education Act of 1902 local authorities were empowered to allocate money for technical education. An important landmark in the 1920s was the development of technical examinations (the Ordinary National Certificate and the Higher National Certificate) and diplomas from the Institute of Mechanical Engineers.

Whilst some pupils did stay on in the higher grades of elementary schools where they could follow vocational or scientific courses, and there were, particularly in London, some trade schools, science schools and central schools, a system of free secondary education for all, end-on to elementary education, was not provided until 1944. Moreover, it was widely assumed that the School Certificate examinations were suitable only for grammar school pupils (and not necessarily for all of those). In 1926 the Hadow Report recommended the setting up of new examination boards to develop and administer new examinations for the increasing number of (non-grammar) secondary schools) (It was not, however, for a further thirty-seven years that this aim was to be realized in the establishment of the Certificate of Secondary Education.)

The Spens Report of 1938 was critical of the way in which having the Higher School Certificate came to be regarded as the 'norm' of good achievement. The Report criticized the Board of Education 'for doing little or nothing to foster the development of secondary schools of a quasi-vocational type designed to meet the needs of boys and girls who desired to enter industry and commerce at the age of sixteen' (Spens Report, 1938, pp.72-3).

When war came in 1939 the provision of free secondary education for all was still not accomplished. Many of Spens' criticisms were re-iterated in the war-time Norwood Report which called for a single-subject, internal examination and a general school report which would be based on internal assessment and would cover the school career of each pupil — a concept similar to that of present day 'profiles'.

The Norwood Report had accepted uncritically the view, based on psychological theories of the 1930s, that there were three types of pupil who would benefit from being taught three separate curricula in three different kinds of secondary school — grammar, technical and modern (Norwood Report, 1943, p.4). These views were embodied in the Education Act of 1944. The Act required local authorities to provide free secondary education for all, end-on to primary education, and to ensure that the education was suited to the age, aptitude and ability of individual children)

The educational reforms which took place after 1944 'were intended to remove some of the stigmas attached to lower-class education, provide a new pattern of opportunity and set education in a framework of improved welfare and social justice' (Lawson and Silver, 1973, p.421). The implementation of the Act resulted, however, in a system which was neither egalitarian nor truly vocational. Relatively few technical schools developed and many of those tended to provide a grammar school curriculum.

The Norwood Report considered that terminal school assessment should not be dominated by the universities and that increased teacher control over examinations should be tried on an experimental basis over a transitional period of seven years. Norwood did not, however, anticipate that teachers in secondary 'modern' schools, who were mostly ex-elementary school teachers, would have control over the examinations, but only 'the élite of the profession' (Lawton, 1980, p.94). These views were broadly supported by the Report of the SSEC in 1947 in which it was argued that all public examinations should be held well beyond the statutory school leaving age so that the majority of pupils (some 80 per cent) should be free from external academic constraints (Secondary School Examinations Council, 1947). Assessment before then, the SSEC suggested, should be by objective tests, the results of which would be entered on a school record. The records and final comprehensive reports from the school should then be used to assist pupils towards further suitable courses of study or appropriate employment.

Thus the non-academic strand of the education system remained free, officially at least, of the major formal examinations even after the establishment of the tripartite system of grammar, technical and modern schools which followed the 1944 Education Act.

General Certificate of Education
The 1947 Report of the SSEC also outlined proposals for a new, single-subject system of examinations, the General Certificate of Education (GCE), with examination at three levels: Ordinary ('O'), Advanced ('A') and Scholarship ('S'). The examinations were to be administered by the existing university examination boards, although initially it was hoped that the new system would become internal and teacher-controlled.

It was intended that candidates would bypass at 'O' level the subjects they anticipated taking at 'A' level; that the 'O' level examination would be taken only by pupils over the age of sixteen; that there would be no group requirements; that the 'S' level would be taken only by those competing for state scholarships (in the days before mandatory awards); that both 'O' and 'A' level would have a 'pass' or 'fail' grade; and that the 'O' level pass would be equivalent to the old School Certificate 'credit'.

In practice the system was modified considerably. Few by-passed the 'O' level and nine 'unofficial' grades developed, although, before the pass/fail concept was abandoned in the late 1970s, these were not recorded on the official certificates issued to successful candidates.

The setting of the 'pass' level at the old School Certificate 'credit' level was an attempt to assuage criticisms that a 'pass' in a single subject was meaningless in comparison with the group requirements of the School Certificate. It meant, however, that about 40 per cent of candidates in each subject failed.

The single subject 'A' level examination attempted to provide for the able sixth-former who wished to pursue two or three subjects in depth. It was not intended to attract large numbers of students, nor to be seen as an all-purpose examination. Whilst 'A' level was not designed solely for those intending to enter higher education, it was taken for granted that its prime purpose was to prepare candidates for more advanced studies. The first 'O' and 'A' level examinations were held in 1951.

The GCE examination, unlike the School Certificate, was not intended to assess the kind of education being provided by schools nor, by its very nature as a single-subject examination, could it ensure a balance of subjects for each pupil. It was unequivocally an external assessment of individual candidates. Although the university examination boards did not intend, and did not want, to shape the secondary school curriculum, this was in effect the result, as universities, the professions and employers, required a particular number or combination of subjects.

Many of those attending the non-selective modern schools (and their teachers and parents) were pressing to be allowed to take the new, nationally-attested, external GCE examinations which increasingly were sought after by employers. More and more modern schools entered pupils for 'O' levels and alternative examinations also proliferated. Pupils could not normally take 'O' levels until they were sixteen, but increasing numbers stayed on past the statutory school-leaving age (which was then fifteen) in order to do so. In 1955 *Circular 289* relaxed the age restriction for entrance to 'O' level but warned that teachers in modern schools should beware of developing GCE courses merely for the sake of prestige (Ministry of Education, 1955).

Educational reports of the 1950s and 1960s

During the 1950s social scientists began to investigate the unequal distribution of educational opportunity and the relationship between previous experience, socio-economic status and educational performance. A series of official reports made suggestions about the curriculum and examinations for non-grammar school pupils

In 1954 the Report of the Central Advisory Council for Education expressed concern at the wastage of talent among those who left school at the earliest opportunity. Shortly afterwards Floud, Halsey and Martin reported on the differential access to grammar schools of children whose parents were in non-manual or manual occupations (Floud, *et al.*, 1956, pp.42-62). The Crowther Report, although in favour of the tripartite system of secondary education being extended to further education, was also concerned about the waste of talent that an excessively élitist system of higher education permitted. Crowther recommended that extended courses should be available for fifteen-year-olds in secondary modern schools and that pupils in the lower half of the ability range of the modern schools should have local or regional leaving certificates. For the majority of pupils, however, external examinations should be avoided unless they too were regionally or locally organized, since they had a 'distorting effect' on the curriculum. In Crowther's view examinations should be 'the helpful servants, not the dominating master' of the curriculum (Crowther Report, 1959).

However, a great many pupils still entered — and many passed — examinations for which, ostensibly, they were not suited. In fact, not only was there pressure from parents and pupils for the opportunity to compete in the 'O' level GCE examinations, but '. . . the status and morale of the school itself became increasingly dependent on how well its pupils did academically' (Broadfoot, 1979, p.40).

By 1955 half the modern schools were preparing pupils for external examinations of the Royal Society of Arts, the City and Guilds, the College of Preceptors and for the more prestigious GCE 'O' level. The modern schools were operating under what Tawney called the 'tadpole' philosophy: the unhappy lot of tadpoles is held to be acceptable because some tadpoles do in the event become frogs (Tawney, 1951, p.105).

In an attempt to rationalize this situation (which was rather akin to the circumstances operating in 1911) the Beloe Committee was established in 1958 to consider secondary school examinations other than the GCE. When it reported in 1960 the Committee recommended a new pattern of examinations for sixteen-year-olds in secondary schools (Beloe Report, 1960). It was suggested that, excluding the top 20 per cent of the ability range who were expected to take 'O' level, the next 20 per cent would be capable of taking the new examination in four or more subjects and that a further 20 per cent might attempt individual subjects. The examinations should not merely be 'O' levels 'writ small' but should be designed specially to meet the needs and interests of pupils in the appropriate ability range.

The examinations were to be different in another respect, in that Beloe attached considerable importance to a major role for teachers in shaping and operating them. Thus the new examinations were not to be dominated by the university boards but were to be largely in the hands of serving teachers, responsible to representative regional examining bodies. Beloe also suggested that there should be a central consultative body associated with the SSEC, to co-ordinate the work of the examining bodies and to promote research. Whilst it was anticipated that the results of the new system of examinations would be useful to employers, Beloe expressed the hope that 'they will treat them as only one piece of evidence amongst others, notably school records'.

The implementation of Beloe's recommendations resulted in the establishment of the Certificate of Secondary Education (CSE) in 1963. There were to be three types or 'modes' of examining: an external examination based on a syllabus drawn up by a regional board; an external examination based on the school's own syllabus; or an examination also based on the school's own syllabus, internally marked but externally moderated. The regional boards were to be controlled by serving teachers. The CSE was to have, officially at least, no pass/fail distinction. One of five grades was to be entered on the certificate. (Performance below grade 5 was not classified.) On the recommendation of the SSEC, in order to gain credibility, the standard of grade 1 was to be made equivalent to an 'O' level pass (rather as the 'O' level pass was considered equal to the old School Certificate 'credit'). This was to be the only overlap between the ranking schemes. Whereas the 'O' level was intended for the top 20 per cent of the ability range, the CSE was aimed at the next 40 per cent. The first CSE examinations were held in 1965.

The new approach to examinations and the curriculum, reflected in the increased teacher influence in the content and assessment for CSE, was accompanied by the establishment, in 1964, of the Schools Council for the Curriculum and Examinations. The Council assumed the functions of the Secondary Schools Examination Council and set out: 'to secure a happier marriage than in the past between the actual work of the schools . . . and the examinations which . . . can all too easily stand in the way of necessary innovation' (Lawson and Silver, 1973, p.444). The CSE, like the GCE, continued the trend away from assessment of *school* towards assessment of *individual pupils.*

Thus since the early nineteenth century, examinations for able pupils developed from, and clearly were influenced by, examinations in the university sector and in the professions. Examinations for the remainder of the school population developed much later but were still influenced, albeit to a lesser extent, by the same model. (See Table 1 for a chronological summary of the main developments in assessment.)

Table 1: Developments in Assessment, 1800-1964

1800	Oxford Examination Statute introduced formal written examinations.
1815	First professional qualifying examinations introduced (by the Society of Apothecaries).
1850s	Competitive examinations established for entrance to the Civil Service, to Sandhurst and to Woolwich.
1857	The 'Exeter Experiment': competitive examinations for pupils from Exeter schools.
1858	Oxford and Cambridge 'Locals'.
1868	Taunton Commission recommended that a central body be responsible for examinations.
1911	Consultative Committee of the Board of Education reported in favour of examinations.
1917	Secondary Schools Examinations Council (SSEC) established. School Certificate and Higher School Certificate proposed.
1926	Hadow Report recommended that new examination boards develop new examinations for non-grammar school pupils.
1943	Norwood Report called for single-subject internal school examinations.
1947	Report of the SSEC proposed the single-subject General Certificate of Education (GCE) with 'Ordinary' and 'Advanced' levels.
1955	*Circular 289* relaxed age restriction on entry to 'O' level.
1960	Beloe Committee reported on secondary school examinations other than the GCE.
1963	Certificate of Secondary Education (CSE) established.
1964	Schools Council for the Curriculum and Examinations founded.

2 The Public Examination System: its strengths and weaknesses

The tripartite arrangements which followed the Education Act of 1944 have now given way to a more comprehensive system. According to the latest official statistics (*Social Trends 16,* 1986, p.205), around 90 per cent of local authority pupils attend non-selective schools — although the 'comprehensive' nature of some of these is questionable (Benn, 1980).

In most secondary schools, at the end of the third year, pupils choose from a range of options the courses they wish to follow during their fourth and fifth years, a procedure which often marks the end of any attempt to implement a 'common' or 'core' curriculum (Chitty, 1980). Over the years, many more pupils than were envisaged originally have attempted at least one subject at GCE 'O' level or CSE level: 90 per cent, rather than the target group of 60 per cent (Nuttall, 1982).

In view of the obvious influence of public examinations on schools and young people it is necessary to be sure of their value.

Functions of public examinations

There are several arguments advanced in favour of public examinations. These arguments are summarized here. Later we shall consider the counter arguments.

Examinations serve a number of functions not only for the candidates but also for parents, teachers, admission tutors and employers — as well as for society as a whole. They provide achievement 'benchmarks' indicating a pupil's success relative to his or her peers. These benchmarks enable all those concerned to receive feedback on pupils' progress and achievement. Research has indicated that the majority of pupils expect schools to prepare them for examinations, even, or perhaps particularly, at a time of high youth unemployment and reduced opportunities (Rutter, *et al.*, 1979; Gray *et al.*, 1980).

The information provided by examination results is more than just teachers' personal views of pupils' abilities: it has the benefit of having been assessed by external examiners with no knowledge of the individual candidates. Where there is a tradition of classroom autonomy, such as is enjoyed by teachers in our system of education, this is important. Well-planned examinations should, therefore, enable the question of whether pupils have attained specific standards to be answered objectively. Ideally, examinations should enable teachers to draw up educational goals, to see to what extent these are being achieved, and to provide valuable feedback to pupils. Public examinations can also serve to increase the motivation of teachers. Increasingly, teachers — and schools — are judged by the examination results their pupils achieve. This information has become available more widely with the implementation of the 1980 Education Act which ensures that schools make public their examination results. The attainment of examination standards provides credentials for employers or, in the case of pupils remaining in full-time education, for admission tutors in institutions of further or higher education.

In addition to these specific purposes, closely linked to the candidates, there are other, broader social functions which it is claimed are, or could be, served by examinations. Nationally-assessed examinations could provide information to enable widespread monitoring of achievement to take place between schools, local authorities and geographic regions of the country. Examinations can provide 'objective' means of identifying and rewarding merit. They can operate, therefore, as mechanisms of social selection. In theory, the system assumes that those most deserving of a higher position in the social order, by reason of their proven ability, are identified and rewarded, and the possibility of nepotism is avoided (Satterley, 1981).

A somewhat different argument is advanced by Hargreaves who suggests that examinations can foster equality of opportunity (Hargreaves, 1982). Hargreaves maintains that during the 1950s and 1960s, with the development of the CSE examination, the increase in pupils taking public examinations was considered to be a way of opening up opportunities, by ending restriction to a grammar-school-type élite and by giving the opportunity for success to those not judged sufficiently able to take GCE 'O' levels. There seems little doubt that many pupils who would not have 'passed' the 11-plus and attended grammar schools under the tripartite system, and others who would have been relegated to the lowest streams, have been able to succeed in the broadened system.

Finally, the examination system can be seen as a source of social control. Examinations provide pupils with a powerful incentive to work, just at the age when they are becoming more resistant to the discipline of school and home, and more susceptible to distractions far removed from study. As Hargreaves suggests, examinations

> transformed an interpersonal problem, of teachers' control of pupils, into an impersonal problem: teachers needed no longer to impose their authority confrontationally, but could appeal to outside forces, the examination board, the pupils' own interests and the value of examinations in the job market, as an incentive to every pupil to behave well and work hard at the school syllabus. And it has worked extraordinarily well for many pupils (Hargreaves, 1982, p.50).

Growth of unease about the system

Almost from the first written papers, public examinations have been the subject of criticism, from individual educationalists, from government officials and committees, from teachers and from researchers. Edmund Holmes, writing in 1911, considered that

> in a school which is ridden by the examination incubus, the whole atmosphere is charged with deceit . . . All who become acclimatized to the influence of the system — pupils, teachers, examiners, parents, employers of labour, ministers of religion, members of Parliament, and the rest — fall victims, sooner or later, to the poison that infects it, and are well content to cheat themselves with outward and visible results, accepting 'class-lists' and 'orders of merit' as of quasi-divine authority (Holmes, 1911, pp.65-6).

The Report of the Consultative Committee of 1911 expressed concern about the negative effects of examinations. In 1938 the Spens Report criticized the dominance of the School Certificate and in 1943 the Norwood Report called for changes in the examination system. Norwood recommended that examination results should be supplemented by a record of the pupils' school career. Similar pleas were made by the Secondary Schools Examinations Council (1947) and in the Crowther Report (1959).

The limited value for employers of examinations as a record of pupil achievement was noted in the Beloe Report (1960). Hard on its heels came the Newsom Report (1963). Newsom's concern for the neglected half of the school population, the average and below-average students, encouraged teachers in their efforts to relate activities, both in and out of school, to students' needs and interests. The unforeseen divisive consequences of some of these efforts have been noted by both Shipman and White (Shipman, 1980; White, 1971).

The Beloe and Newsom Reports paved the way for teachers to be given more responsibilities for co-ordinating examinations. To a certain extent this has lessened the gap between teaching and examining, although the change has related mainly to CSE. Increased teacher-involvement with 'O' levels has been slight.

Criticisms of the dual system

Despite changes that have been made — the increased range of option syllabuses, more teacher-involvement in Mode 3, the introduction of CSE and the removal of the pass/fail classification at 'O' level — there have been many criticisms levelled at the GCE/CSE system. These criticisms are particularly concerned with the structure and organization of examinations, and with the limitations they have imposed on the curriculum, on teachers and on pupils of *all* abilities.

As we have noted, 'O' level GCE and CSE together were originally designed for only 60 per cent of the whole year group. However, pupils could be classified in this notional 60 per cent for one subject and in the lower 40 per cent (i.e. the non-examination group) for other subjects. Some subjects, such as English Language, have always had an entry rate considerably higher than the notional target. Other subjects, such as physics, have a much lower entry rate.

Even so, that the examination system has not been able to provide for *all* sixteen-year-olds has remained a distinct limitation. This became more obvious with the advent of comprehensive schools on a large scale and with the raising of the school leaving age in 1972/3. In the days of widespread selective education, when only about a quarter of pupils attended the examination-oriented grammar schools, most others left school at the age of fifteen. After 1973, it became more essential to provide *all* pupils with a worthwhile record of achievement. Yet Burgess and Adams calculated in 1980 that well over three-fifths of pupils left school at sixteen without achieving a grade A to C at 'O' level or a CSE Grade 1 in any one subject (Burgess and Adams, 1980, p.6). They further estimated that only one pupil in twelve received a certificate which implied 'substantial performance in half or more of the range of subjects taken during their compulsory schooling'. This meant that a sizeable proportion of the age range each year was likely to be considered, and to consider itself, an educational failure since the examinations were, in the vast majority of cases, the only record of assessment used.

Reliability

The lack of reliability in examination grades has been investigated by the Schools Council (Schools Council, 1979). The conclusion reached was that any grades awarded should be considered plus or minus the next (grade). Thus, a candidate obtaining a grade B result should accept the possibility that their paper might have been worth either a grade A or a grade C. In addition, the marking of some subjects may be more prone to unreliability than others. For example, the judgement of an essay answer in English or social studies usually is considered to be more difficult to make than the judgement of a mathematics problem.

There is also the difficulty, faced by chief examiners, of ensuring that standards remain as uniform as possible. Individual examiners may be subject to fatigue, change of mood or 'script saturation' (Fagg, 1983).

Comparability

Even if perfectly reliable systems of marking could be developed, however, problems of comparability would remain. Given the number of examination boards, subjects and syllabuses, it is hardly surprising that a given grade in one subject may not be comparable exactly to the same grade in another subject or even in the same subject in another board or mode. Goldstein has argued that the goal of comparability between boards is unrealistic, and this view is supported by the preliminary results of a study carried out by the ILEA (Goldstein, 1982).

Some subjects are considered to be harder than others. Forrest showed that it was comparatively easy to do well at 'O' level in English Language and English Literature, art, biology and geography, whereas history, mathematics, French, chemistry and physics were more difficult (Forrest, 1971). These findings were broadly confirmed by Nuttall, Backhouse and Willmott (1974). In the CSE Mode 3 there was also a possibility that, despite attempts at external moderation, some schools did permit more lenient marking than others.

Examination board officers do their utmost to ensure that standards remain as constant as possible, yet the problem of gauging the difficulty of questions, and the need to collate different syllabuses, place statistics of previous grade distributions in a very influential position (Orr and Nuttall, 1983).

Norm base

The examination system we have become used to operating has been criticized for being limited by its dependence on a norm base. In other words, roughly the same proportion of pupils gained each grade each year. As Broadfoot has pointed out, a pupil's sense of failure may be artificial since external examinations are subject to the influences of this norm base, which makes it quite inevitable that a high proportion of pupils will gain low or unclassified grades, whatever the standard of teaching or learning (Broadfoot, 1980).

The question of whether boards rely too heavily on a norm base is difficult to answer. Clearly examination board officers would be foolish to ignore results from previous years. Chief examiners, however, have a duty to attempt to impose absolute standards. The establishment of norms for 'A' levels by the SSEC in 1960 has served as the basis for 'A' level grading for over twenty years (see Table 2 below) (Joint Matriculation Board, 1983).

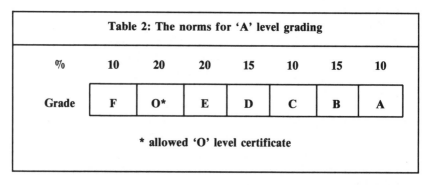

Table 2: The norms for 'A' level grading						
% 10	20	20	15	10	15	10
Grade F	O*	E	D	C	B	A
* allowed 'O' level certificate						

In fairness it must be said that these percentages were meant to be regarded only as a guide. However, national statistics show that, for large entry subjects, the pass rate has remained very close to the 70 per cent given in the SSEC guidelines. According to Orr and Nuttall, this does not prove that examination boards rely heavily on these norms but, they argue,

> It seems inconceivable that almost exactly the same proportions, but of several times the number of candidates from a much wider range of educational institutions, should attain the same level of performance in the 1980s as in the 1950s (Orr and Nuttall, 1983).

Problems in the grading of GCE 'A' level examinations have been discussed by the Joint Matriculation Board (JMB). The Board recognizes that the shape of the distribution of marks on which the grades are imposed is an important factor in determining the usefulness of the grades . . . When the marks of candidates are bunched towards the centre of the distribution, grading decisions become more difficult to make: a small number of marks will, of necessity, span a grade (Joint Matriculation Board, 1983).

For example, in 1982, in twenty-five of the thirty-four JMB 'A'level examinations with large entries, the number of marks separating B from D ranged from 6 per cent to 3.5 per cent, and in chemistry (Syllabus A) the difference was under 3 per cent.

Cooper claims that, in many subjects, the marking error (or the differences between examiners) is wider than the difference between grades C and D (Cooper, 1981). This situation, as Smith has argued,

brings untold misery every year to very many university aspirants who hope and expect to get B grades and in fact get Ds — thereby instilling deep sense of failure for what might only be a difference of three marks (Smith, 1983).

Competitive base
Public examinations have always been highly competitive. In 'A' level, as has been noted, about 30 per cent of candidates normally fail. In 'O' level about half of those entered have obtained only D or E grades, or have been unclassified. The scripts of these candidates have been judged in comparison with those of other more 'successful' entrants. Those living in poor housing, without the usual amenities, with parents (or single parent) worried about money, have had to compete with others who have experienced considerable advantages including, if deemed necessary, extra coaching in particular subjects. Not surprisingly it appears that, in general, candidates from disadvantaged circumstances systematically do less well than their more advantaged peers (Mortimore and Blackstone, 1982).

Cost
A further criticism is that any examination system is expensive to operate. It could be argued that, at a time of shrinking educational resources, money would be better spent on books. There is in addition a further cost, time. At least two years are spent preparing for all these examinations — time which could be used perhaps for a broader range of activities.

Admission policies

Schools have always varied considerably in their examination admission policies. Some have entered weaker candidates with only a slight chance of gaining a classified grade. Other schools have attempted to maintain a higher success rate by entering only those candidates with a good chance of doing well. There has also been variation in the type of examination for which pupils have been entered. In some schools a majority of pupils have become candidates for the CSE examination and only a few have been encouraged to enter for the more prestigious 'O' levels. For many pupils and teachers, the decision as to which examination to study for has been a very difficult one to take.

Table 3: G C E 'O' Level entries 1982*

BOYS			GIRLS			Total
		%	%			Entries
		0	100	needlework		16467
		3	97	cookery		49313
		26	74	sociology		52979
	(34)	32	68	(65) music		18316
		36	64	biology		234671
	(34)	37	63	(66) commerce		37212
		38	62	rel. sts.		72478
		38	62	german		50763
		40	60	french		157690
		42	58	english literature		249957
		43	57	art		129695
		46	54	eng. lang.		511972
		49	51	history		132404
		50	50	gen.sci.		6316
maths	(60)	53	47	(40)		324664
geography		55	45			193860
economics		58	42			43144
chemistry	(65)	60	40	(35)		145725
computer sts.	(71)	69	31	(29)		33264
physics	(77)	73	27	(23)		183395
tech. dr.		95	5			60921
design & tech.		96	4			14264
woodwork		98	2			14716
metalwork		99	1			12515

Table prepared by Martin Grant

*Where a shift of more than 1 per cent has occured since 1980 the percentage for boys and for girls for that year is shown in brackets.

Sex differentiation

As we have seen, a differentiated curriculum becomes generally acceptable and is widespread from the third year in the vast majority of comprehensive schools. Although all pupils are apparently offered the same choices in most option systems, what happens in practice is that pupils are encouraged to make 'choices' more associated with their sex, race and class than with their level of attainment. Table 3 (on previous page) shows how gender stereotyping is reflected in the entries for the GCE 'O' level examinations in 1980 and 1982.

Effect of examinations on the curriculum

There has long been a concern that teachers' adherence to an examination-dominated curriculum may have negative effects on their teaching. The report by H.M. Inspectorate for Schools (HMI) on secondary schools in England and Wales found that the style and quality of work in the fourth and fifth years of secondary schools were dominated by examination requirements (Department of Education and Science, 1979). Teachers, knowing that their effectiveness was likely to be judged in terms of examination results, tended to adopt teaching styles they considered necessary to promote examination success. This tended to encourage teaching which, in the view of H.M. Inspectorate, was 'unsound, unstimulating and ineffectual'. Moreover, this restricted kind of teaching may result in the limited learning which, some critics claim, is all that most examinations, in particular those which are timed tests, are able to measure.

These and similar criticisms have been reiterated by a variety of interest groups in evidence given in 1982 to the House of Commons Select Committee on Education, Science and the Arts, which enquired into the curriculum and public examinations in the last two years of compulsory schooling. In their evidence the Confederation of British Industry (CBI) complained about the over-academic nature and content of many syllabuses and called for more emphasis on the application of knowledge and skills to real-life situations and on the ability to listen and speak effectively. The Society of Education Officers criticized out-of-date syllabuses which were more concerned with content than with learning objectives (Geddes, 1982).

Selection

Examinations are justified partly on the grounds that they are useful for selection to further and higher education and for employment. Yet there are some studies which have shown that their predictive value is questionable (Entwistle and Wilson, 1977). Broadfoot argues that 'the function of public examinations, to provide for selection and maintain public confidence in standards, takes precedence over educational consequences' (Broadfoot, 1980, p.276).)

Examinations have, of course, affected selection lower down the secondary school, either into separate streams aimed at 'O' level or CSE, or, more commonly, into separate sets. This has been viewed by many as an unwelcome extension of the old 11-plus division of pupils into secondary modern or grammar schools. Once in a CSE stream, it has proved difficult for a 'late developer', or a pupil whose ability has been wrongly assessed, to transfer, the difference between the examination syllabuses being simply too great.

Self-esteem

Relegation to the CSE groups or below, the rigid ranking of examination grades and the high failure rate could all have a damaging effect on pupils' self-confidence and esteem. These issues have been discussed in more detail in the literature on labelling, expectation and the self-fulfilling prophecy (Lacey, 1970; Lacey, 1974; Hargreaves, 1967; Brophy and Good, 1974). Perhaps the most disturbing criticism of the whole system is the claim by Burgess and Adams that examinations do little even for those who do well in them. This, they maintain, is because examinations 'test mostly the lowest category of performance, that of "isolated recall" or plain memorizing' (Burgess and Adams, 1980, p.6), and because they neglect vital human skills and qualities such as an enquiring mind, persistence, co-operation and creativity.

Conclusion

This chapter has listed the strengths and the weaknesses of the public examinations system. The strengths are considerable: the establishment of benchmarks useful for pupils, teachers, parents and employers; a strong influence on the motivation of pupils and teachers; and a structure for the organization of learning which, at best, enables pupils and teachers to co-operate in striving for legitimate goals. However, as we have argued, there are also a number of weaknesses. The dual system has been criticized for being too narrow; aimed only at a limited target — and therefore unsuitable for a comprehensive system; unreliable and unable to ensure that grades are comparable; unduly limited by the influence of annual 'norms'; over-costly; and finally, and perhaps most ironically, unable to cater adequately for even the most able pupils.

These two perspectives on examinations are not completely contradictory. Our view is that, whilst changes in the current system are clearly needed, some kind of structured system which provides feedback through the use of established benchmarks is essential. A later section of this paper will review attempts made to reform examinations and will make suggestions for change.

3 How Are Pupils Assessed in Other Countries?

Since there is widespread dissatisfaction with the public examination system in this country it may be helpful to review how pupils are assessed in other countries and to consider what may be learnt from them. Clearly it is not possible to describe numerous education systems in detail. The political and educational objectives of other countries vary considerably and detailed information in English is not always readily accessible. From those countries for whom evidence is available, we have selected three: Sweden, the United States and France. Sweden and the USA are particularly relevant comparisons with England and Wales because they represent well-established comprehensive systems of secondary education. The comparison with France may also prove valuable since, relatively recently, France has changed from a selective to a common system of schooling — at least for the years of compulsory attendance.

Sweden

Education in Sweden is compulsory from the age of seven to sixteen. The basic comprehensive system *(Grundskola)* has three stages. From the age of seven until they are ten, children attend the junior level *(Lågstadiet);* from eleven to thirteen, the middle level *(Mellanstadiet);* and from fourteen to sixteen, the senior level *(Högstadiet).* The post-compulsory, tertiary sector is also comprehensive and incorporates the former traditional, academic *gymansium;* the long-established vocational schools *(yrkeskolor);* and the newer continuation schools *(fackskolor),* into one *Gymnasieskola* (Boucher, 1982).

The curriculum, general guidelines and methods are set out in the government's *Läroplan 80 (Lgr 80),* officially introduced in 1982. While stressing the importance of basic knowledge and skills, the document rejects passive recall and emphasizes active learning at all stages of education.

On entering the middle level at the age of eleven, pupils follow a common curriculum with special provision only for those with learning difficulties. However, at the senior level small homogeneous ability sets may be created in certain subjects, but they cannot operate for more than a year and the composition of any group may not be the same for more than one subject. In the last two years of compulsory school students can choose to take some subjects at a more advanced level. About half the age group do so.

Since the implementation of *Lgr 80* teachers are required only formally (for recording purposes) to grade pupils in years 8 and 9, that is, in the final two years of middle schooling. The elimination of selection at eleven has long since removed the need for official grades at the junior level but, Boucher claims, informal grading on a 1 to 5 scale is a regular, albeit unofficial, feature of the middle stage. In addition, pupils take standardized achievement tests on seven occasions between the ages of nine and sixteen. Although these tests are voluntary, about 90 to 95 per cent of pupils take them. The purpose of the tests in the early years is mainly to establish the position of a particular class in relation to similar classes throughout Sweden, although they also serve a diagnostic function for individual pupils. This assessment is not intended to be subjective although at least one commentator has claimed that, despite the use of published criteria, teachers have considerable latitude in assigning marks (Neave, 1980). During the final three years, in senior school, the tests serve a rather different purpose and students are awarded grades on a scale of 1 to 5. These grades are particularly important in the final year for ensuring entry to the students' first choice of course (they are called 'lines' in Sweden) in the tertiary institutions.*

Following a government inquiry in 1976, tertiary education in *gymnasieskola* is available to virtually all those who want it. However, it is the system which is open and tertiary, not individual institutions. Not all *gymnasieskola* offer the same lines and some lines and institutions are more sought after than others. Consequently, whilst in theory access is

---

*In the country as a whole there are about twenty-three different lines structured within three broad areas of study: arts and social studies; economics; and science and technology. Lines may last for two, three or four years. Shorter lines tend to have developed from former vocational or continuation schools, longer ones tend to have developed from the traditional academic or technical gymnasia.

open, to enter a popular line or institution students will need to have earned higher than the average 2.5 grades in class 9 in the senior school, since the grades are effectively used for selection in the increasingly (albeit informal) competitive tertiary market (Boucher, 1982). Mallinson has described some of the strategies adopted by students in order to cope with this situation (Mallinson, 1980). Some deliberately do badly in the class 9 assessment so that they can repeat the year. Others, having initially chosen more difficult courses, revert to easier courses in the final year in order to maximize their chances of a higher grade.

Changes in expectation, in admission policies and in employment patterns over the past decade, and particularly since 1976, have meant that virtually all sixteen-year-olds apply for a place in a tertiary institution. About 90 per cent are offered places and 85 per cent take them up. The remaining 15 per cent who leave the full-time education system at sixteen are predominantly those with low grade levels in class 9, who are also from low socio-economic groups. In order to encourage re-entry, work experience is taken into account and can bolster low grades when older ex-students apply for admission.

The grading system has been criticized and attempts have been made to abandon it altogether. Recommendations to this effect were made in 1977 in the report of the government's commission on marking which suggested a leaving certificate which stated what curriculum a pupil had followed. How well a pupil had performed would be judged by means of termly meetings between teachers, parents and pupil at which behaviour and welfare would also be discussed.

France

Education in France is compulsory from the age of six to sixteen. From the age of six to about eleven children attend primary school *(école primaire)*. Following government decrees in 1964, a selective secondary system has gradually been replaced by a streamed comprehensive system. Since then pupils have attended comprehensive lower secondary schools *(collèges uniques)* from twelve to sixteen. From sixteen to eighteen those remaining in full-time education attend different kinds of upper secondary schools *(lycées)*.

Despite the further reforms of 1975 (the 'Haby' reforms) which attempted the introduction of mixed-ability teaching, stressed the non-cognitive aspects of education and widened the concept of individual records of achievement, the system which has evolved is increasingly differentiated beyond the second year of the *collèges* (Broadfoot, 1982; Neave, 1980).

Pupils follow a core curriculum in the primary school (repeating grades if necessary) and for the first two years (the *'cycle d'observation'*) of the *collèges*. At the end of this two-year period, despite the Haby reforms, approximately a quarter of the pupils are diverted from mainstream education (Passmore, 1983). They either embark on vocational courses in the *collèges* to prepare for a three-year course in a vocational school or they enter vocational schools directly. They will then study for the *Certificat d'Aptitude Professionel* (CAP) (roughly equivalent to a City and Guilds qualification in Britain). In theory it is possible, but in practice it is very difficult, to return to mainstream schooling. A recent report in France is highly critical of these vocational schools, arguing that young people there are in a cul-de-sac, being trained for the kind of employment which is fast disappearing (Legrand, 1983).

The final two years of *collège* is known as the *'cycle d'orientation'*. At the start of this period only about two-thirds of pupils are still following the general course. Of the remainder, those not in vocational courses or schools are repeating the year in order to get on to general courses or to pass the time until they can start apprenticeships. (About 5 per cent drop out at this stage.) Those pupils following general courses are placed (on the basis of an assessment of performance agreed by teachers, a guidance counsellor, doctor, psychologist and parent representative) in either 'A' or 'B' classes. 'A' classes have a faster pace and provide the opportunity for the study of a classical or second modern language. 'B' classes work at a slower pace and have a greater emphasis on core subjects (Dundas-Grant, 1982). Pupils in both groups are expected formally to prepare for entry to the upper secondary level (although some leave at sixteen to seek employment or apprenticeships).

The majority of these pupils take the college-leaving certificate whether or not they intend continuing their education. Formerly this certificate was a regionally-administered external examination, the *Brevet d'Etudes du Premier Cycle* (BEPC), but it is now a comprehensive record of achievement. The record is compiled by teachers and can be challenged by parents, in which case a committee arbitrates.

Most of those remaining on general courses until the age of sixteen will receive at least two, probably three more years full-time education in the 'upper cycle' of secondary education. What kind of education this is depends on their performance in the BEPC, the kind of *lycée* they go on to and the *Baccalauréat (Bac)* course on which they enrol.

Some students enter vocational schools to follow courses leading to a variety of technical diplomas or to the *Brevet d'Enseignement Professionnel* (BEP). About 40 per cent of the age group enter *lycées* to study for the *Bac*. The several different kinds of *lycées* — general, technical, 'polyvalent' (covering general and technical subjects) — form 'a subtle hierarchy of prestige' (Corbett, 1983). Similarly there are more, or less, prestigious *Bac* courses.

The courses are in eight sections (A to H). Top of the hierarchy are the mathematics and physics-based *Bacs* (the 'C' series). These are usually required for entrance to the two-year preparatory class for entrance to the *Grandes Ecoles,* France's most prestigious institutions of higher education. Parents make strenuous efforts to get their daughter or son into a *lycée* with a record of good *Bac* results. Schools attempt to maintain high levels of results by 'squeezing out' weaker candidates or by making them repeat a year before allowing them to take the examination. About 40 per cent of the age group take the *Bac*. About 28 per cent of the age group are likely to succeed and most of these will go on to some form of higher education. There is, however, growing concern in France over the effects on the comprehensive philosophy of a single examination which is virtually the school-leaving certificate for those who remain in the school system to 18 or 19. There are pressures to extend the methods of continuous assessment used lower down the system.

United States

Comprehensive schools developed in the United States as early as the 1920s (Marklund, 1981). This development was part of a conscious attempt to develop a sense of national unity and homogeneity in a new and ethnically heterogeneous country. American schools usually have twelve grades through which pupils pass from the age of six to eighteen. From six to eleven pupils are in grades 1 to 6 of *elementary schools*. From twelve to fourteen they are in grades 7 to 9 of *junior high schools* and from fifteen to eighteen they are in grades 10 to 12 of *senior high schools*. Increasingly, however, some states are combining junior and senior high schools.

Until relatively recently, pupils would be awarded grades (A, B and so on) by their teachers for course work and, when final-year pupils graduated from high school, they would be issued with that school's diploma. There was no national, regular system of assessment. During the 1970s, however, there was increasing concern expressed by both the general public and the school boards over whether schools were providing value for taxpayers' money; over a supposed lowering of standards of work and behaviour; and over the laxity of (so-called) 'progressive' educational ideas and methods. There was concern that the graduation diplomas 'certified twelve years' attendance but not necessarily the ability to read, write, add or multiply' (Cookson, 1978). The situation in the States appears complicated to those used to the British system because school boards do not fit the traditional party political structures, although they are made up of elected officers. Both the school boards and the individual state legislatures have a right to comment on the education system. In many cases pressure for more systematic assessment has come from the legislature rather than from the boards (Burstall and Kay, 1978).

Two kinds of testing are common. The first, such as that carried out by the National Assessment of Educational Programs (NAEP) is concerned with the performance of the system (rather like the Assessment of Performance Unit of the DES). The second kind is concerned with the performance of individuals. Minimum Competency Tests (MCTs) have been developed mainly by commercial organizations (such as the Iowa Tests of Basic Skills) and have been adopted by a number of states. Forbes argues that the emphasis has switched recently from system evaluation to individual evaluation using MCTs (Forbes, 1982).

Depending on whether the focus of testing is the system or individuals, there is wide variation between states in the subjects or courses chosen, in the age of pupils and whether an entire cohort or only a sample is tested (Burstall and Kay, 1978). For example, in California all pupils are tested in the first, second and third grades and then only twice more, in the sixth and twelfth grades (these last two being the final grades of elementary and secondary schooling). In Colorado only a sample of fifth and eleventh grade pupils are tested, whilst in Washington DC all grades from 1 to 9, but no other pupils, are tested. Most states test their twelfth-grade pupils and a few even attempt to track down those students who have dropped out. The most frequently tested grades are the fourth and eighth (age nine and thirteen) and not, as might be expected, grades 6 and 9 from which pupils transfer from one stage of schooling to another. In some schools assessment is on a state-wide basis, in others it is organized within a school district.

Most assessments cover mathematics and verbal skills although others cover writing, civics and 'basic life competencies' (for example, form-filling). Other schemes attempt to assess a wide range of educational goals, such as personal and social development and attitudes, although the technical problems of finding satisfactory instruments of measurement are severe. Some schemes, such as the Michigan Educational Assessment Program (MEAP), are closely related to the traditional curriculum subjects — at least until the final grade assessment which is more concerned with 'life role competencies'.

Students wishing to enter university are encouraged to take the Scholastic Aptitude Test (SAT) offered by the College Board. This was developed by the Educational Testing Services (ETS) to ease the difficulties of selection for higher education using only the school-assessed high school diplomas. Entrance to the more prestigious universities is generally dependent on high SAT scores. Fears over declining standards were fostered by the gradual lowering of the average scores being achieved in the SAT (National Commission on Excellence in Education, 1983a). As a result of this concern the College Board has initiated the 'Education Equality' project to identify and enumerate the basic skills needed for college entrance. Following a conference in St Louis in 1981 groups of educators have been drawing up guidelines for schools to aid the acquisition of basic skills in such areas as reading, writing, numeracy, and scientific thought. To these 'basic' competencies have now been added six 'basic academic subjects' including English, the arts and a foreign language. The project 'may give the United States the nearest thing it will ever have to a core curriculum' (David, 1983).

The National Commission on Excellence in Education, appointed by the Secretary of Education in 1981, carried out an investigation into the state of education in the USA. The Commission's report is highly critical of the 'cafeteria-style curriculum in which the appetisers and desserts can easily be mistaken for main courses' and the tendency to treat 'minimum competency' as the finishing tape rather than the starting blocks of educational attainment (National Commission on Excellence in Education, 1983). The report recommends a compulsory core curriculum in five basic areas for those seeking a high school graduation diploma; that more time be spent in studying at school and at home; that standards of teaching be raised and teachers' salaries, conditions and accountability be improved; and — of immediate relevance to this discussion — that 'standardized tests of achievement (not to be confused with aptitude tests) should be administered at major transition points'.

What lessons can be drawn from these three systems?
The problems of direct comparison between educational systems of different countries with their varying social, economic and political

contexts have already been alluded to. With that caveat in mind what lessons might we learn from Sweden, France and the USA? Three points emerge clearly. First, each of the the three systems has a greater proportion (indeed a majority of the age group) participating in post-compulsory education from sixteen. This suggests that most students feel it worthwhile to do so. Second, none of these systems places as much emphasis on public examinations during the years of compulsory schooling as do England and Wales. Sweden and the USA have no such examinations and in France students do not face external public examinations until the academic *(Bac)* or vocational examinations *(BEP)* at the age of eighteen or nineteen. Third, each system has alternative forms of assessment: Sweden has teacher-awarded grades, diagnostic tests and individual profiles; France has individual records of achievement and a degree of parent involvement; and the USA has continual assessment by teachers.

The three systems are not, it must be said, problem-free. Sweden still retains a marked social class bias in entrants to the tertiary *gymnasieskola* and about 8 per cent of the age group drop out of education before sixteen (*The Times Educational Supplement,* 1983, 4 February). France, despite laudable intentions of reform, still sifts the non-academic from the academic students relatively early on, and continues to do so throughout the system. America, in striving for minimum-competency, is in danger of holding back able pupils, of whom inadequate further demands are made, and of subjecting the less able to fruitless repetitive attempts at achieving narrow minimum goals (Cookson, 1978; Houts, 1977). The education systems of these three countries undoubtedly could be improved further but in terms of emphasizing skills and qualities which cover a wide spectrum and are assessed over a considerable period of time; of encouraging students to continue in or return to education; and of opening rather than closing educational doors leading to increased opportunity, they could be our mentors.

4 Alternative Forms of Assessment: profiles and graded assessments

The three systems of education described in the preceding section each make use of assessment procedures other than formal written examinations. Within this country much recent interest has been shown in pupil profiles and graded assessments.

The notion of detailed school reports, covering the many aspects of pupil careers, is not new. As early as 1943 the Norwood Report recommended that 'an account of the pupil's school record' should be entered on a certificate of examination performance (Norwood Report, 1943). Three years later a report of the Secondary School Examinations Council stated that, on leaving secondary school, every pupil should have 'a comprehensive school report containing the fullest possible positive information about him and his abilities and potential' (Secondary School Examinations Council, 1947). The same theme was reiterated in 1959 when the Crowther Report argued that some of the purposes of an external examination could be met by an assessment 'of a pupil's performance and attainments during his whole time at school' (Crowther Report, 1959). Similarly, three years later the Beloe Report called for systematic school records to enhance the value of, and diminish the dangers of, external examinations (Beloe Report, 1960).

Nearly forty years after the publication of the Norwood Report dissatisfaction with the narrowness of examinations persists, yet progress towards implementing these earlier recommendations and developing detailed pupil records has been slow. Recently, however, interest in pupil records has revived. There are several reasons for this. Thousands of sixteen-year-olds leave school with no public examination certificate. These young people have no formal recognition of their experience and attainments, or of their personal qualities and potential. Many of these pupils are 'early leavers', departing from school at Easter or shortly before the examination season. Some are not entered for any examination and a few are entered, but gain no classified grades. Not surprisingly, these pupils tend to be those with least confidence in their ability, who are easily discouraged by failure. Moreover, their failure is all the more obvious, now that all pupils stay on in statutory full-time education until the age of sixteen.

The growth of youth unemployment, of skill-centred further education courses, of work-related youth training schemes and of courses 'bridging' school and work has also served to highlight the need for more detailed pupil information. Moreover, it is generally recognized that many personal qualities are valued by employers and that these, and certain skills, are not reflected in the single grade of an examination result (for those who have taken public examinations) or in the brief, often stylised, personal testimonial which, for many, has been the sole alternative.

Profiles

Alternative procedures for recording personal development and achievement are now quite numerous. Their characteristics (for no two are identical) are listed by Broadfoot and they are referred to frequently by the generic term 'profile' (Broadfoot, 1982a). Mansell defines this term as 'a set of data recording the scores of a student in respect of his performance over a range of items' (Mansell, 1982a). Although 'profile' can be used as a term to describe purely academic items (as in a detailed breakdown of scores),* more usually the term refers to a wide range of cognitive and non-cognitive developments. (Throughout this section the term 'profile', unless otherwise stated, is taken in its broadest sense to include records of attainment, personal achievement records, etc.)

Of the several different profile schemes now in use in schools only a selection will be described here. In the further education sector there have been a number of recent developments in profiling by the City and Guilds of London Institute, the Royal Society of Arts and the Business and Technical Education Council (Further Education Unit, 1982; Further Education Unit, 1984). Moreover, within the more open course structure of FE, profiles are perhaps more able to influence the curriculum.

One of the earliest schemes to be developed, and one of the few to

---

*See for example the School Mathematics Project (SMP) Course III, the Hertfordshire Mathematics Achievement Scheme and the School Mathematics Individual Learning Experience (SMILE).

have been evaluated independently, is the Swindon Record of Personal Achievement (RPA) (Stansbury, 1980). From this developed later the Record of Personal Experience (RPE). They were started in schools in Wiltshire and Devon, in 1970 and 1973 respectively, and both are now used by schools outside these counties. The stated aim of the RPA is the development of personal qualities. When the scheme was devised it was envisaged as an alternative accreditation system for 14 to 16 year-olds who were unlikely to sit for external examinations. However, it was also seen as an appropriate target for pupils throughout the entire ability range and, in some cases, it was offered to every pupil in the fourth year. Both RPA and RPE are pupil-directed and consist of records compiled personally by pupils over a period of about two years. Neither scheme is an assessment procedure since marks and grades are not awarded. Pupils keep a diary and loose-leaf record cards. Their entries are discussed and validated each week with the RPA/RPE tutor and some items are transferred to a loose-leaf record book. The record book is seen as 'a declaration of identity' which can be used during interviews for employment or for post-school education (ibid.).

Personal Achievement Record
The Personal Achievement Record (PAR), developed by staff at an Evesham School in 1979, is also pupil-directed. Although initially designed for average and below-average pupils, fifth formers of all abilities can opt to keep a PAR log-book and about 75 per cent do so (Duffy, 1980). The log-book has three sections. The first section lists the school courses followed (with results of any attainment tests and eventually, examination results). The second section contains a sixty-item check list divided between the four areas in which employers are likely to be interested: language, mathematics, practical skills and social skills. The third section is based on 'personal achievement' in sporting, leisure or community activities.

When pupils consider they have mastered an item on the list they ask an appropriate teacher to check and record this achievement — the principle being that 'pupils must initiate and staff must confirm statements of fact' (ibid.). Whilst there have been attempts to make each item sufficiently specific for validation, almost inevitably in a list of fifteen items per skill area, some are more nebulous than others. (For example, in the area of mathematics skills, 'Can measure accurately', and in the area of personal social skills, 'Can organize his/her work efficiently'.) Pupils aim to complete the log-book by Easter and it is then taken to interviews with prospective employers, many of whom (at least in Evesham) helped initially to develop the PAR check list and to finance the scheme.

Scottish Council for Research in Education (SCRE) Profile

The SCRE profile assessment system was developed and piloted extensively by the SCRE in conjunction with a working party of Scottish headteachers (Scottish Council for Research in Education, 1977). In contrast to the previous examples, the profile is teacher-controlled and teacher-assessed. It has a four-point grade scale. Assessments are made on the basis of the year group rather than the class group, in order to provide maximum comparability both within and between schools. There are two methods of recording data: a manual and a computerized system. The SCRE profile has three main sections: basic skills, performance and work-related characteristics.

The pupils' school leaving report is a condensed summary of the profile information. It provides a description of the pupils' basic skills, personal qualities (only positive information is included), involvement in formal and informal school activities, as well as more traditional ratings for subject achievements. The principal difficulties associated with the scheme are the complexity of the assessment pattern, the high cost of materials and the need for considerable in-service training.

Sutton Centre Profile

The Sutton Centre Profile differs again because it not only includes teachers' comments on all aspects of pupils' school life and work, but it is intended that both pupils and parents respond. The pupil is seen as 'the centre of a dialogue between teacher and parent, as well as being a party to it' (Fletcher, 1980).

In summary, it is apparent that there is, as yet, no clear pattern in profile schemes currently in use in schools. Some are summative and are little more than an efficient testimonial whilst others are formative and provide the opportunity for systematic monitoring of progress and for diagnostic recommendations from one year to another, across phases of educational provision. Some include pupils as a key member of the assessment team and encourage them to take an active role in their learning. Others remain teacher-controlled.

Evaluation of profiles

Although the notion of individual records is not new, the design and implementation of profile systems is a more recent development, dating only from the Swindon initiatives in the early 'seventies. Consequently, few of the existing schemes have been evaluated independently.

The Schools Council's evaluation of RPA was published in 1979 (Swales, 1979). It was found that the RPA motivated pupils and helped them to organize their ideas and their work, and pupils of limited ability had a source of achievement and pride. However, the scheme tended to be confined to the less-able fourth and fifth formers which lowered its prestige so that it suffered from low status and lack of recognition by some pupils. Employers were not closely involved and were uncertain of the value of RPA for their purposes. Moreover, pupils with problems of literacy were at a disadvantage since the record relied heavily on pupils' own entries.

The Schools Council carried out a survey at the request of the Secretary of State, to assess the extent to which profile schemes were in operation (Balogh, 1982). All local authorities in England were involved. Schools were identified whose profiles met four research criteria: the profile recorded skills and qualities other than traditional attainment; the information was systematically presented; the profile was not a confidential document sent direct to potential users; and it was available to all pupils in the specified target group (though not necessarily to all pupils).

Only twenty-five schools across the entire country met these criteria. Most had introduced profiles (their own or a modification of existing models) in order to 'recognize the non-examination aspects of school life' (ibid.). Few reported any resulting changes in the curriculum. When nine schools were studied in greater depth it was found, not surprisingly, that few viewed profiles as an alternative to examinations, although this may reflect 'a pragmatic rather than a philosophical stance' (ibid.). Some schools reserved them for the 'less able', thus risking the devaluation of profiles for pupils and employers alike. Some teachers expressed ethical unease over assessing and commenting on items such as 'honesty', 'perseverance' and 'punctuality'. This is interesting since the first two are the kind of personal qualities for which profiles could be seen as an ideal means of communication and, with the third item, are likely to be of interest to employers. The teacher's unease does, however, indicate the problems of subjectivity noted below. Similar resistance, at both teacher and local authority level, was subsequently reported by the author of a second Schools Council study (Goacher, 1983).

Difficulties of profiles
A number of reservations have been expressed about the desirability of profiles as a means of assessment. There is concern that if profiles are used only for pupils not taking (or not expected to do well in) public examinations, then they are likely to be seen as suitable only for the 'less able'. In these circumstances the very possession of a profile may be used as evidence of low ability or become what one headteacher has termed 'the National Certificate of Incompetence' (Goacher, 1982). If, however, profiles are concentrated on a rather narrow range of skills thought suitable for employers' needs, they are in danger of neglecting another important function — that of providing the diagnostic information increasingly important in selection and guidance in post-school education and training (Doe, 1981).

Questions have also been raised about the subjectivity of profile records. If assessments in either cognitive or non-cognitive areas are to be referenced against the norm, what is the basis for the norm? Is it the class, the school or the age group as a whole? If, on the other hand, assessment is to be criterion-referenced, can criteria be defined in all areas with equal validity or without reference to supposed norms? It has been suggested that the use of a numerical-rating system of recording 'may lend an air of objectivity to a subjective system' (Worly and Bird, 1982). Moreover, different teachers may assess the same behaviour quite differently. (Rutter, *et al.*, 1979).

Some have queried whether teachers are equipped — or even justified in attempting — to assess personal qualities (Jackson, 1982a). Do teachers of large numbers of classes know pupils sufficiently well? Is it possible fairly to judge pupils in the context of a school that they may be only too anxious to leave? Pupils' attitudes and behaviour may reflect the school ethos rather than any immutable personality traits and 'the same individual may be transformed at work and it is questionable to blight their chances with old emnities' (Doe, 1981). There is a danger, too, that teachers' subjective judgements may be more exposed than those of examination markers to the biases of social situations, to the influence of the 'halo' effect, to social class stereotyping or to misinterpretation (Broadfoot, 1982). Some work on these issues and on the possibility of assessing what may be called 'the affective domain' has been carried out under the auspices of the Scottish Council for Educational Research (Dockrell and Black, 1978).

An additional consideration is the time (and to a lesser extent the cost) and the administrative difficulties involved in maintaining detailed and accurate profiles. The volume of information generated for each pupil could become unwieldly and unusable. Teachers may spend too much time on the completion of records, time which arguably could be spent more profitably on actual teaching (Jackson, 1982a). In Scotland it was found that the operation of the profile scheme placed staff and resources under considerable strain, particularly in the small number of schools which also took part in the Affective Domain Project.

Advantages of profiles

There are also a number of arguments in favour of profiles. A carefully constructed profile could, for instance, help to motivate pupils. In the Schools Council's survey on their use pupil motivation was mentioned by teachers as being their most valuable consequence (Balogh, 1982). Attributes such as dependability, initiative, co-operation and sociability, recognized as being useful assets in the labour market, are able to be developed and assessed in some of the more encompassing profiles. The role of the school in encouraging achievement — other than the strictly academic — and in redressing the balance between academic and practical aspects of the curriculum, can be highlighted in a pupil's profile (Worly and Bird, 1982). Furthermore, if schools are obliged to provide the means and opportunities for the acquistion of what Raven calls 'life-useful competencies', the curriculum of the fourth and fifth years will have to be broadened (Raven, 1977). Schools could benefit considerably from this process.

Employers, further and higher education staff and training personnel are able to gain useful information and insight on applicants (Scott-Archer, 1982). In addition, the more diverse and different style of comment on a profile which has been built up over time could encourage a trend away from the frequently sterile platitudes of school reports. Different teachers will make contributions throughout the pupils' career and these may off-set or complement one another, so that the final profile can be more valuable than current testimonials which too often represent the retrospective view of one teacher.

If the profile system were to include — as do the Swindon RPA and RPE schemes — some element of pupil direction and pupil self-assessment, it could provide excellent opportunities for pupils to develop skills of critical self awareness and self confidence. While most advocates of profiles do not see them as being incompatible with certification, 'they cannot be aggregated or conflated into a simple grade of pass or fail. They have to record successes as well as failures, strengths as well as weaknesses' (Mansell, 1981).

There is considerable support for the development and introduction of profiles both within and beyond the education system. (Many of the most interesting developments have taken place in the further education sector and have been pioneered by the FEU.) A policy document produced by one teacher union recommends profiles for all school leavers, a view supported by the Chief Inspector for H.M. Inspectorate (National Association of Schoolmasters/Union of Women Teachers, 1983; Browne, 1983). The CBI, in evidence to the Select Committee on Education, Science and the Arts 'strongly supported' them, as did the MSC and the TUC (Balogh, 1982). The Labour Party has stated that it would like to see a national system of profiles for all young people (Labour Party, 1982). The Liberal/Social Democratic Party (SDP) alliance also favours their introduction. The Conservative Government has acknowledged the value of profiles although as a complement to, not replacement for, examinations (Department of Education and Science, 1981).

There remain, however, several unresolved issues which need to be considered.

Teacher and pupil preparation

At present teachers receive little initial training in the skills needed to monitor and assess a wide range of skills and attributes. Subsequent in-service professional development is equally poorly served. Few local authorities have an adviser, and few schools have graded posts with special responsibility, for this area. The confusion and difficulties encountered, therefore, in deciding which areas to evaluate, of developing new skills of assessment, and of ensuring compatibility and fairness have been described graphically by Goacher (Goacher, 1983). Similarly, if pupils are to play an active part in the construction and maintenance of their own profiles, and there is some evidence that this could be a means of sustaining their motivation and self-esteem, they too need help in developing necessary skills and insights (Balogh, 1982). The need both for more pupil involvement and more teacher openness to alternative techniques is stressed by Goacher.

Technical considerations

As already noted, there are a number of technical considerations concerning measurement that need now to be addressed. At a theoretical level these considerations have been discussed, and the need for action research highlighted, by Nuttall and Goldstein (1984). The question of comparability between assessors — already raised with regard to current public examination — needs a thorough investigation. Similarly, the reliability of one teacher's judgement over a time period also needs to be estimated. This will be difficult since the non-cognitive aspects of development may show a greater variation than cognitive ones and any reliability trial will have to take this into account. Finally, the validity of measures used in any profile must be examined.

A national or a local profile?

An additional concern is whether profiles are best produced and used locally, or whether they should have national currency. Would there be any means of ensuring inter-school, regional or national comparability? Would it be desirable to do so? In Balogh's view it would be unwise to prescribe the content of profiles but rather they should be developed in relation to local needs and after consultation with teachers, parents and pupils. (To these could be added local employers and MSC training personnel.) Much depends on who are considered to be the potential users of profiles. If profiles are to be used predominantly for average or below average pupils, expecting to enter local further education or youth training schemes, then locally developed schemes, responsive to local needs, could be more appropriate. If, however, as seems more equitable and desirable, profiles are to be used for all pupils, some nationally agreed criteria (though not necessarily a national format) would seem to be necessary. Suggestions along these lines have already been put forward by Burgess and Adams (1980). They outline proposals for a three-stage programme, nationally validated, for all pupils, from the end of the third year to the end of the fifth year.

Graded assessments

Graded assessments (sometimes known as graduated, or criterion-referenced tests) provide another alternative to current methods of examinations. They are assessments based, not on set proportions of candidates gaining particular grades, but on the achievement of specified levels of skill, regardless of age. Each grade is intended to cover a certain amount of knowledge up to a defined standard. Pupils can progress by the 'mastery learning' of a grade at a time and, together, the grades form a progressive sequence, although not all pupils would expect to pass all grades.

Pupils entering for graded, criterion-referenced assessments can be given clear information about the skills needed in order to do well. If a candidate has not yet gained the necessary degree of skill or has not mastered the knowledge specified, entry can be delayed. Rather than entering a norm-based examination with unspecified criteria and a considerable risk of failure, pupils can, if necessary, take longer to prepare for a more explicit, criterion-referenced assessment and enter with a greater chance of succeeding. Norms may be utulized in assessment construction, however, so that a high proportion — say 90 per cent — of entrants are able to pass a particular grade.

Probably the best known graded assessments are those which have been used for over a century by the Associated Board of the Royal Schools of Music. (In 1980 there were over 350,000 candidates for the Board's eight grades.) Graded assessments are also used widely in school sport, under the auspices of the British Amateur Gymnastics Association (BAGA). Only relatively recently, however, have they been used in any core subject of the secondary curriculum — notably in the field of modern languages (Graded Objectives in Modern Languages — GOML) (Harding *et al.*, 1980).

Advantages of graded assessments

The advantage of the GOML scheme (and of graded assessments in general) is that 'it is progressive, with short-term objectives leading on from one to the next; that it is task-oriented, relating to the use of language for practical purposes; and that it is closely linked into the learning process, with pupils or students taking the tests when they are ready to pass' (Harrison, 1982). (GOML and music grade examinations have pass rates of approximately 90 per cent and 80 per cent respectively.)

Short-term graded objectives allow the assessments to be designed from the bottom up rather than from the top down. Many more pupils, therefore, are able to enter for at least some of the grades. It is also possible for graded assessments to be designed for a particular curriculum.

Of course, it must be recognized that some subjects are more suited to a graded assessment approach than are others. Learning a language or a musical instrument is, perhaps, particularly suited to this method, whilst English literature or history are, at first sight, less so. (Music tuition, for example, is often on a one-to-one basis.) It is also true, however, that these subjects are less suited to more traditional examination methods. This does not mean that assessment is not possible. Mitchell has described how, at least in the first three years of one secondary school, all courses can be assessed by criterion-referenced mastery grades and personal achievement grades (Mitchell, 1982).

Advocates of the modern language schemes — of which there were 58 in 1981 — claim that pupils have become better motivated and teachers more enthusiastic (Harrison, 1982; Balogh, 1982). It is also claimed that more pupils choose to study modern languages in the fourth and fifth years of schools using graded assessments in these subjects. Motivation is probably increased by the frequent positive reinforcement of success at each grade, rather than the five year, long-term deferred gratification of 'O' levels or CSEs taken at one 'sitting' in the fifth year. Graded assessments have also generated a high degree of enthusiasm amongst teachers. This is probably related to their involvement in local schemes, the feeling of being in control rather than acting as passive agents of examination boards, and the benefits of teaching more motivated pupils (Nuttall and Goldstein, 1984).

Unresolved issues

As with all innovations, graded assessments have a number of potential problems. Their use might result in an excess of testing, with some of the undesirable consequences noted by commentators on the American educational scene (Sherwood, 1978), although a recent review of current methods of assessing pupils in schools and LEAs has shown that many methods of dubious value are already used extensively (Gipps *et al.,* 1983).

Comparability between different versions of assessments which are dependent on teacher involvement and — in theory at least — so flexible in terms of when they can be taken may also be difficult to achieve. Problems of validity and reliability also need to be resolved. To switch from an unreliable examination system to an unreliable graded assessment system, even if this could be justified on educational grounds, would be unfortunate.

The involvement of classroom teachers in the development of methods of assessment takes time and may itself cause difficulties for schools. For instance, in Harrison's survey even committed teachers admitted to problems of organization and time in dealing with individual rates of progress (Harrison, 1982). For the sake of expediency they had to resort to assessing all pupils at about the same time. This practice, compromising as it does one of the key principles of mastery learning, was criticized by H.M. Inspectors in their report on graded tests in Oxfordshire

(H.M. Inspectorate, 1983).

Crucial questions must also be asked about the use to be made of graded assessments. If their principal use is formative — that is as a means of providing regular feedback on progress and diagnostic help to teachers — then questions of comparability and reliability, although important, may not be so critical. If, however, the main use is summative — providing a definitive statement of pupils' skills and attainment — then, in order for employers to give currency to the results, the reliability, validity and comparability issues cannot be avoided.

Finally, there is the potential problem that the targets for graded assessments may be limited. Since the Cockcroft Report on mathematics recommended the development of 'graduated' assessments, the DES has initiated a programme of research and development (Cockcroft Report, 1982). However, this is directed principally towards the 40 per cent of pupil's deemed 'low attainers', rather than across the board. In our judgement this is a grave mistake. Such a 'two-class' system of assessment would be even more unhelpful than the present GCE/CSE divide. The very reinforcement of learning and motivation that a graded system provides could be distorted only to reinforce the lower status of those pupils engaged in the scheme. There is some evidence that other progressive innovations such as the social education courses of the 1960s or the Record of Pupil Achievement pioneered by Stansbury have led to the institutionalization of differences between pupils (Shipman, 1980; Swales, 1979).

The challenge

The challenge for the developers of profiles and graded assessments is to devise assessments which not only motivate pupils, rather than turn them off, but which are also sensitive and efficient. Another challenge is to design a system which has a common structure for all subjects and yet, within that structure, allows freedom to be flexible. Thus it may be helpful to have a *set* number of stages and *fixed* periods of assessment whilst allowing quite different forms of assessment for different subjects. In mathematics and modern languages, for instance, timed papers may be appropriate. In English, a collection of different pieces of work — some of which may be self-edited pieces of writing — may be more suitable. An exhibition of work may be appropriate for craft, design and technology and so on.

A further challenge is to provide a means of maintaining cohesion for pupils involved in a variety of different forms of assessment at different times of the year. One solution might be to use pupil profiles as a course guide to a programme planned by pupils and their teachers.

An additional advantage of such a system would be that the current debate over the balance between a common curriculum and options could be resolved. All common core subjects could be taken to a fixed level, whilst options — allowing increased depth (higher grades) in some areas, and increased width (new subjects at lower grades) — would also be available. Furthermore, assessments in integrated curriculum areas such as the humanities and in methodologies (the investigative procedures) could be provided.

The use of graded assessments would, however, have considerable implications for school organization. The current system of peer cohorts, moving up through the years, would provide a poor context for assessments based on 'readiness'. At present, holding back pupils for a year because they are deemed 'below par' can be emotionally upsetting and may have negative effects on pupils' subsequent motivation. However, in the system we are proposing, the wholesale moving up of age cohorts would not be the norm. Where *teaching* groups were commonly of mixed ages and where pupils followed courses on the basis of individual achievement in graded assessments (or perhaps where older students were changing direction and beginning elementary courses) the relationship of age to achievement would lose its significance. Many schools already deliberately arrange mixed-age pastoral tutor groups so that pupils get to know those from different years. The situation could be reversed so that pastoral tutor groups were homogeneous in age but some teaching grops were not. The wide age range of candidates in music grade examinations, of Open University students and adult education students, and the increasing participation of adult students alongside school pupils in classes in community schools, suggest that greater age differences in groups in 11-18 secondary schools (or 11-16 schools and 16-19 tertiary colleges) are unlikely to be detrimental and may be advantageous to pupils. Timetabling would, however, be much more complex, calling for greater emphasis on individual progress.

As ideas, such methods are attractive: they focus on success rather than failure; they involve teachers and — in the case of profiles —pupils in assessment; and they have diagnostic functions. What is now needed is careful development so that the statistical foundations of these methods may be well laid.

5 Reform of the System: proposals and outcomes

Over the past thirty years a number of proposals for reforms of the public examination system have been put forward. Few of the reforms, however, have been aimed at redressing the criticisms of the system reported in the preceding sections. In fact, concern has stemmed less from specific criticisms of the principle of an externally-validated examination system aimed at the most able 60 per cent, than from pressures of organizational change in schools, demographic changes in school populations, and social changes relating to the world of work.

Some of the reforms suggested, and some which have been implemented, have been little more than piecemeal 'tinkering' changes at the fringes of the system. Thus, the concept of pass/fail at 'O' level has given way to a grading system and there has been some attempt at developing alternative modes of assessment (with more school involvement). However, it has already been noted that the numbers involved in GCE 'O' level Modes 2 and 3 have been relatively small. Other proposed reforms have been concerned with the restructuring of the 18-plus examination; the introduction of an examination for the seventeen-year-old age group; and the merging of the two 16-plus examinations ('O' level and CSE).

Each of these proposed reforms has encountered stiff opposition from interest groups wishing to preserve, or only alter slightly, the status quo. Although these groups have at times included teacher organizations and other groups, the strongest resistance has come from the GCE boards and, in particular, from the universities. Right from the inception of school examinations the universities have been closely involved with the system by their (admittedly fluctuating) representation on the SSEC; by their power to impose university admission criteria linked to examination passes; by their traditional links with sixth forms; and by their involvement with, and influence over, the university examination boards.

Examinations in the sixth form

As soon as it began work in 1964 the Schools Council devoted considerable attention to examinations in the sixth form. There were two main reasons for this. First, expanding numbers entering the sixth form included many pupils for whom a two or three-subject 'A' level course as a stepping stone to university or the professions was not ideal. Second, there was growing concern at the early and narrow specialization in sixth-form work. This concern was, in fact, shared by the universities and voiced by the Standing Conference on University Entrance (SCUE).

The SCUE suggested, in 1966, that the sixth-form curriculum should be based on a modular structure with students selecting a 'package' usually of two 'major' and four 'minor' subjects. These proposals were set out in the Schools Council *Working Paper 5* and further modified in *Working Paper 16* which recommended that more detailed work be carried out (Schools Council, 1966; Schools Council, 1967).

To this end the Schools Council and the SCUE set up, in 1968, two joint working parties on the sixth-form curriculum and examinations. One, chaired by Professor Butler, was to be primarily concerned with those pupils intending to enter university. A second working party, chaired by Dr. Briault, was to be concerned with those pupils who did not intend to enter university — and with the relationship of the curriculum to further education, industry and commerce.

'Q' and 'F' proposals

In December 1969 the two working parties presented a joint statement on what came to be known as 'the Butler-Briault proposals' for the Qualifying ('Q') and Further ('F') examinations (Schools Council and Standing Conference on University Entrance, 1969). It was suggested that a broader five-subject curriculum could be designed, with candidates taking up to five subjects at 'Q' level after one year in the sixth form and studying three in greater depth, 'F' level, in the second year of the sixth form. The 'Q' level examinations were to be marked by the CSE boards and the 'F' level by the GCE boards. The working parties also suggested that 'O' level should include what they termed 'in-school attestation' of pupils by teachers. This was to be a form of teacher assessment which would reduce the dependence on an external examination.

The Butler-Briault proposals encountered much opposition from the universities, the examination boards and the teacher unions (Binyon, 1970). The universities, although on balance opposed, were not unanimous. They had, after all, been among the campaigners for a reduction in early specialization and they had deplored both the swing away from science, and the mutual ignorance of the arts and science sixth-former. However, debate about the broadening of the curriculum invariably returned to the link between 'A' level standards and university entrance. Many universities were concerned that a five-subject sixth-form curriculum would dilute the quality of current 'A' level studies and — by implication — of university entrants. Their comments to the Schools Council, therefore, revealed deep divisions and reservations about the (necessarily) untried nature of the proposed examinations; about their accuracy in identifying potential university students; and about the suitability of the 'Q' examination for both the general sixth former and the university aspirant. (Interestingly, some of the universities opposed the 'Q' examination on the grounds that the 'liberating experience' of the first year in the sixth form would be destroyed by preparing for more public examinations. *The Times Educational Supplement,* 19 July, 1970.)

The powerful GCE examination boards, to which the universities had long since delegated the administration of the examinations but which had only one representative on the Schools Council, also put forward strong opposition. They claimed that they formed the group most concerned with examinations, yet they had the most to lose if the 'Q' and 'F' proposals were to be accepted. It was feared that the adoption of 'Q' and 'F' would mean that 'A' levels would fade out. Further, both the proposed in-school attestation at 'O' level and the increased teacher participation in 'Q' and 'F' would reduce the work of the boards. Along with many university academics, the boards objected to the paucity of research evidence available to support the proposals. Not surprisingly, the CSE boards were more favourably disposed towards 'Q' and 'F' since the teacher-assessed 'Q' examination would validate the teacher-assessed CSE (Binyon, 1970).

The teacher unions, well represented on the Schools Council, were more divided. Whilst there was some support for the proposals, the National Union of Teachers (NUT), after initially favouring change, argued that the curriculum proposed for the 'new' sixth form was not sufficiently broad.

Finally, the SCUE itself — from whose ranks one of the working parties had been drawn — expressed the fear that, if 'O' levels at sixteen were to remain, the introduction of 'Q' and 'F' would entail candidates sitting for three public examinations in three successive years — a situation the committee considered educationally unwise and unfair.

The Butler-Briault proposals were rejected, therefore, by the

Governing Council of the Schools Council in July 1970 and the working parties were sent away to prepare plans which would be acceptable to all parties. (It is interesting to note, in passing, that at the same meeting the Council suggested merging the GCE and the CSE into a joint examination at 16-plus — a suggestion which has taken many years to implement.)

Despite the rejection of the 'Q' and 'F' proposals there was widespread agreement on the need for a broader sixth form course. 'In the 1980s' wrote one commentator, 'the specialist sixth will be a memory, part of the history of education' (Jennings, 1970). Having been sent back to the drawing board, the working parties drew up plans for two more new examinations.

'N' and 'F' proposals

The Schools Council *Working Paper 46* and *Working Paper 47* put forward proposals for examinations at Normal ('N') and Further ('F') levels (Schools Council, 1973a; Schools Council, 1973b). The suggested structure had two tiers. Pupils would start a two-year course in five subjects, the 'N' level. In the second year of the course some pupils would choose to do additional work in two of the subjects, which would be examined at the 'F' level. It was considered that, together with the Certificate of Extended Education (CEE) (see p.60), the 'N' level would meet the needs of the broader spectrum of abilities in the new sixth form and that the CEE and the 'N', together with the 'F' level, would widen the curriculum and avoid early specialization and restrictive subject choice.

A four-year programme of research and surveys was undertaken to assess the feasibility and implications of the proposals. From the pilot case studies the Joint Examinations Council Sub-Committee concluded that schools could devise an educationally satisfactory sixth-form organization within the existing levels of teaching resources and physical accommodation (Schools Council, 1978).

The 'N' and 'F' proposals and the feasibility studies received mixed responses (Schools Council, 1980). The universities were again among the strongest critics. Despite the full participation of the SCUE in initiating 'N' and 'F', not one university gave unequivocal support. Whilst many of them expressed sympathy with the underlying principles and with the difficulties faced by schools, it was considered that the proposals did not provide an appropriate solution (Standing Conference on University Entrance, 1979). Most of the criticism centred on the implications for the universities of the proposed changes. The probability of larger teaching groups and the subsequent danger of 'teacher overload' were seen as detrimental to prospective university entrants. It was feared that the broader subject range (five subjects) would lessen the knowledge in specialist subjects currently acquired by entrants who had studied three 'A' levels in depth. Whilst professing to favour a broadening of sixth-form work the universities were not prepared to sacrifice subject depth, since this carried the implication that degree courses might need to be extended in order to compensate — a step to which the universities could not commit themselves. It is interesting that some of the staff of the newer, technological universities or those teaching relatively newer subjects (such as social sciences) were more inclined to favour the proposals, whilst some of the older universities expressed misgivings about the lowering of standards (Schools Council, unpublished papers).

In their concerted response to the Schools Council the universities summarized their position thus:

> The foremost aim must be to continue to meet the national need for well educated and highly trained graduates, which in turn depends on the advanced level of the education provided for the more able sixth formers; to preserve the high standards that this demands it is essential to maintain a proper academic challenge for the more able boys and girls at all stages of secondary education (Schools Council, 1980).

The universities reaffirmed their 'commitment to school examinations at 18-plus and their confidence in GCE boards as the appropriate bodies to be entrusted with responsibility for standards (Standing Conference on University Entrance, 1979).

Whilst all the GCE examination boards opposed the 'N' and 'F' proposals, some (for example the Southern Universities Joint Board and the Cambridge Board) were more overtly hostile than others. They saw the introduction of 'N' and 'F' as taking more time, expense and administration (Schools Council, unpublished papers). Others (for example, the Oxford and Cambridge Schools Examination Board) recognized the need for change (Oxford and Cambridge Schools Examinations Board, 1978).

A decision on the 'N' and 'F' proposals was delayed by the change of government in May 1979. The new Secretary of State for Education (Mark Carlisle) expressed his intention of retaining 'A' levels as the benchmarks of high achievement. The Schools Council, however, were asked for their views on provision for the rest of the 16 to 19 year-olds.

In December 1979 the Council put forward proposals for an Intermediate ('I') level examination aimed at students with GCE 'O' level Grade C or above (or CSE Grade 1) and designed to occupy about half 'A' level study time over a period of two years.* The Council considered that the 'I' level, plus the Certificate of Extended Education (CEE) for students of the next level of ability, would provide for all non-'A' level sixth formers. It was thought that an 'I' level would broaden the sixth-form curriculum for those students who might find 'A' level too academic or too restricting, and who might otherwise leave school after two years in the sixth form with nothing to show for their labour.

In a Consultative Document of October 1980 the Government expressed interest in an 'I' level examination limited in the range of subjects and restricted to candidates taking at least two 'A' levels at the same time (Department of Education and Science, 1980). It could, the document suggested, 'artistize science subjects and scientize arts subjects'. However, it was emphasized once again that the standard of 'A' levels for university entrance must be maintained. No further decision has been taken about 'I' level, although some spark of interest has been re-kindled by a recent statement by the former Secretary of State (Sir Keith Joseph) at the Head Masters' Conference (*The Times Educational Supplement,* 7 October, 1983).

Certificate of Extended Education and the new 17-plus

The debate on how best to provide for other groups in the 'new sixth form' had continued alongside the 'Q' and 'F' and the 'N' and 'F' controversies. At the same time proposals for raising the school leaving age to sixteen were gaining support and sixth forms were continuing to increase in size and ability range. When the Butler-Briault proposals were first published the National Union of Teachers (NUT) issued a policy statement pressing for 'the establishment of an additional examination on the lines of an "Extended CSE", specifically designed to cater for the needs and aspirations of these "new sixth formers"' (National Union of Teachers, 1970). Under pressure from the NUT the Governing Council of the Schools Council passed a resolution to that effect in July 1970.

---

*Proposals for an intermediate level examination were first made by the Parliamentary Committee of the Headmasters' Association in 1968 (Duckworth, 1975). The proposals became submerged in the subsequent discussions of and proposals for the CEE.

Several suggestions were put forward as to which target groups any new examination should be aimed at. In general it was believed the target should be those not intending to follow degree courses and in need of alternatives to 'A' level. In 1972 the Schools Council presented for discussion options for different target groups (Schools Council, 1972). It was suggested that if the group were too wide there would be a danger that a new examination might become an automatic 'staging post' for all sixth-formers, including those en route to university who would then face three public examinations in three years. If the target group were too narrow it could be confined to the 'less able', or to those who wanted an examination of a standard mid-way between 'O' and 'A' level.

Further consultations between the Schools Council and the CSE boards resulted in proposals for a Certificate of Extended Education (CEE). This was designed to provide a one-year, five-subject course in the sixth form for those who had obtained CSE grades 2 to 4. The Schools Council Working Party suggested that feasibility studies be carried out on pilot examinations. A number of such examinations were developed by the CSE boards and some formal recognition was given in 1974. The Secretary of State, however, refused to underwrite any CEE certificates issued by the CSE boards. Instead the boards had to issue a CSE certificate with CSE grades to which was attached a 'letter of credit' explaining what the CEE grades would have been! (Foster, 1983)

Whilst most of the GCE boards expressed some support for the CEE, two rejected the proposals outright. Moreover, the remaining boards voiced doubts about the feasibility studies, about whether standards would be maintained and about the wisdom of introducing an examination at 17-plus without changes being made at 16-plus and 18-plus (Schools Council, unpublished papers). The CSE boards were more favourably disposed towards the results of the CEE trial examinations, although shortcomings in the feasibility studies were noted.

In May 1976 the Schools Council submitted to the Secretary of State for Education (Fred Mulley) a recommendation that the new examination be established mainly for those sixth formers with only modest achievements at sixteen. However, neither Fred Mulley nor his successor, Shirley Williams, was prepared to introduce the CEE whilst new examinations at sixteen were being discussed, or without better evidence of its acceptability to employers and teachers, including those in further education. Instead, in 1977, Shirley Williams set up a committee, led by Professor Keohane, to study the proposals. The Keohane Committee consisted of representatives mainly from schools, further education, industry and commerce, trades unions and local government.

In its Report the Keohane Committee supported the Schools Council's proposals in principle but with certain reservations (Keohane Report, 1979). It expressed the opinion that the Council's proposals for a single-subject examination gave no guidance about the balance or nature of the courses and did not include basic communication skills, numeracy or vocational preparation. Keohane argued that, since many of the target group (17-plus, having achieved CSE grades 2-4) would be aiming to seek employment, the courses should reflect more accurately these needs and those of employers and should be more in line with courses offered in colleges of further education.

Keohane stopped short of requiring CEE candidates to follow a strictly vocational course or of altering directly the single-subject course to one consisting of a balanced group of subjects. But he did suggest that schools should consider combining the single-subject CEE with programmes which contained elements of basic skills, including social skills, vocational preparation, and careers education. Keohane recommended that the Secretary of State should initiate immediately the development work necessary to introduce the CEE along these lines and, in the interim, continue the pilot CEE.

The view of the incoming Conservative administration, following the 1979 general election, was that the CEE was of little value. Consequently it was decided that the CEE should not to be recognized by the DES and that the pilot examinations should be phased out (Department of Education and Science, 1980). The Government considered that moderate-ability sixth formers, who hoped to leave school for employment at seventeen, needed a vocationally oriented course which would provide a qualification acceptable to students and to employers. In October 1980, therefore, the Secretary of State (Mark Carlisle) issued a consultative Green Paper which stated the Government's intention of developing a new pre-vocational examination available in both schools and colleges for the same target group of seventeen-year-olds (Ibid.). According to the Green Paper, the GCE and CSE boards would not be involved in the development of the new examination but would concentrate instead on the development of a single system of examining at 16-plus. The Government thus appeared to reject the experience gained by the boards in operating the pilot CEE examinations.

The Green Paper was influenced by a report from the Further Education Unit (FEU) of the DES entitled *A Basis for Choice* (Further Education Unit, 1979). This report advocated a curriculum structure which stressed 'flexibility, transferability and currency'. A well-defined common core was suggested, with more flexible general and specific vocational studies. A profile system was advocated as the most appropriate form of assessment but nationally agreed criteria were deemed necessary for national validation.*

The sentiments of *A Basis for Choice* were echoed by a subsequent report on *Vocational Preparation,* also from the FEU (Further Education Unit, 1981). The report proposed that vocational preparation should be available to *all* school leavers but, in the short term, particularly to those not able to benefit from conventional academic or vocational training. The report also suggested that vocational preparation required a programme 'based as much on the self-perceived needs of each young person' as on the needs of professionals and employers. As in *A Basis for Choice,* assessment by profiles was advocated.

The future of certification at 17-plus was held in abeyance for almost two years, during which time the economic circumstances of the country changed considerably. Youth unemployment rose to unprecedented levels and the Manpower Services Commission (MSC) extended its sphere of influence with the development of the Youth Training Scheme (YTS). Uncertainty ended in May 1982 with the publication by the Government of its proposals for a new 17-plus qualification (Department of Education and Science, 1982). The Government statement considered that, for this age group, most single-subject examinations did not have a sufficiently practical slant, nor did they necessarily have suitable syllabuses and form the basis of a coherent programme. Moreover, there was a confusing array of award-giving bodies (such as the Technical Education Council, the Business Education Council and the Royal Society of Arts) acting independently of each other. The Secretary of State, Sir Keith Joseph, announced, therefore, the introduction of a new range of pre-vocational courses to be offered in schools and colleges of further education. This would lead to the award of a national certificate.

The new pre-vocational qualification, the Certificate of Pre-Vocational Education (CPVE), has been designed to provide 'comprehensively and coherently' for the 16-19 age group. It was intended that the implementation of the CPVE would be co-ordinated with the education and training programme for the YTS so that 'common objectives may be covered by the same syllabus'. The CPVE syllabuses would 'give a vocational bias to a balanced programme of general education'. The new certification would be administered by a consortia of further education boards, the

---

*See discussion on profiles p.43

GCE and CSE boards and local authority associations. There would be no pass/fail distinction but each certificate would represent assessment across a wide range of the work covered.

Overall, the notion of the new 'voc' has been favourably received by the FEU, the further education sector and the MSC. There have, however, been criticisms and reservations. Some of these have been accepted by the Government and the CPVE has been modified accordingly. For example, students on 'caring courses', initially excluded, have now been included. But arguments over who should administer the examination, over membership of the consortia, and over representation and participation of schools relative to further education colleges, have taken longer to be resolved. There have been wranglings over whether or not to include teacher representatives on the administering body and accusations that the new examination is being pushed out of the school sector into further education (*Education,* 1983). The whole programme is now administered by the City and Guilds of London Institute (CGLI) and the Business and Technician Education Council (BTEC) through the new Joint Board for Pre-Vocational Education established in May 1983.

Some commentators see the concept of a common core curriculum for the CPVE as too narrowly based, ignoring the more imaginative, cross-disciplinary approach of *A Basis for Choice* (Mansell, 1982). Other observers complain that CPVE provision ignores certain groups, such as the least able and those students who used the almost defunct CEE as a stepping stone towards 'A' levels (Hedger, 1982). Although a possible link with the MSC/YTS has been generally welcomed as a move towards more unified and comprehensive provision for seventeen-year-olds, there have been anomalies and difficulties over payment and certification of participants (Jackson, 1982; *The Times Educational Supplement,* 1 April 1983).

Shortly after the introduction of the CPVE in September 1985, a document was published by the FEU evaluating the 1984/85 pilot schemes. This showed that around 40 per cent of the 896 students participating in the schemes had dropped out before the end of the course, a loss largely attributable to employment, with at least a third of all students leaving at some stage or other to take up jobs as a direct result of work experience. At the same time, student perceptions were found to be very positive. At least 70 per cent of those interviewed said they would recommend the CPVE to their friends, and 80 per cent considered that the programme had assisted them with their career plans. Tutors, for their part, felt that the CPVE was very relevant to employment prospects — giving students the confidence, relevant vocational skills and work experience to achieve their objectives (Further Education Unit, 1985).

Clearly, CPVE was introduced partly to replace the plethora of existing qualifications with one recognizable label. Yet this laudable notion has already run into difficulties. A recent BTEC circular (86/35) announced the introduction of a 'first award' system for those 16-plus-year-olds 'who have made a rational and informed choice of a career route' and 'are of technician potential'. This is in direct competition with the CPVE and threatens to undermine the concept of one credible qualification offering routes to further education and training. Those most likely to favour traditional qualifications and experience will probably opt for the relatively familiar BTEC award; while those who choose to take the CPVE may well be required to spend an extra year working for the BTEC 'first award' *before* moving on to mainstream vocational provision.

The Government is now attempting to rationalize post-16 vocational provision with the announcement in July 1986 of the setting up of a National Council for Vocational Qualifications (Department of Employment, 1986). The Council will not run its own examinations or tests but will accredit other bodies' qualifications provided they fit the criteria of a new National Vocational Qualification. The Department of Education and Science will be responsible for briefing the new body on educational issues, but overall control will be with the Department of Employment.

Examinations at 16-plus

Alongside debate over the reform of examinations in the sixth form, controversy over the possibility of merging GCE 'O' level and the CSE into a joint 16-plus examination has continued.

A single system of examining at 16-plus was suggested by the Schools Council as early as 1970 (only five years after the introduction of the CSE). In 1971 the Council presented plans for a new 16-plus with the target date of 1977. It was argued that 'a common system should be based on the view that the curriculum comes first . . . the examination system must serve the schools, not dominate them' (Schools Council, 1971). The Council drew attention to the fact that the notion of a continuum of ability had gained ground in recent years and that this made it undesirable, if not impossible, to prejudge pupils' development and to classify them into 'CSE types' or 'GCE types'. Moreover, the growth of comprehensive schools and the proposed raising of the school-leaving-age made a two-tier examination system inappropriate.

Under the auspices of the Schools Council, feasibility studies were undertaken and in 1974 trial examinations were taken by nearly 70,000 candidates. The target date for the introduction of a joint 16-plus was moved forward to 1980. The Schools Council received comments on the feasibility studies from all the GCE and CSE boards, from teacher associations, subject associations and from the further education sector — but from only two universities. This last point is somewhat surprising since, in commenting on the 'N' and 'F' proposals, the SCUE had stated that, in view of the implications of a common examination for the development of the sixth-form curriculum, 'the universities wish to maintain a strong influence in school examinations at 16-plus' (Standing Conference on University Entrance, 1979). The two universities which did comment saw no reason to alter the existing system (Schools Council, 1973).

Whilst none of the GCE boards opposed the proposals, none gave unqualified support. Most of the CSE boards accepted the principle but claimed there was confusion over whether a common *examination* or a common *system* was being proposed. The University of Cambridge Local Examinations Syndicate wrote that 'inadequate evidence from the studies revealed more problems in a single system than in the dual system' (Cambridge University Local Examinations Syndicate, 1976).

Once again the question of the maintenance of standards arose. It was argued that if the 16-plus were to be too easy for able candidates there would be a danger of lowering of standards at 18-plus and, by implication, of university entrants. The Cambridge Syndicate, whilst expressing sympathy with schools' difficulties in administering a dual examination system at 16-plus, did not think the system should be scrapped unless there was 'convincing evidence' that a new system would be better. That evidence was judged to be lacking. Concern was expressed that the proposed 'federal structure' (groups of examination boards operating on a regional basis) would weaken the power of the present university-linked boards to guarantee standards.

Both the Oxford Delegacy and the Southern Regional Examinations Board were, on the whole, confident that the experimental examinations in French, history and physics were appropriate for pupils of a wide ability range, although they differed on the need to discriminate at the top end by using papers of graded difficulty (Oxford Delegacy of Local Examinations and the Southern Regional Examinations Board, 1976). However, the Oxford Delegacy expressed fears about making decisions on the basis of only one-year trial examinations; about the extra burden greater involvement would place on teachers and the more varied syllabuses on awarders; and about the insufficiently demanding nature of the examinations for more able candidates wishing to pursue their subject to a higher level. (Optional papers for both ends of the ability range were suggested.) About half the teachers' groups favoured a single system and about a quarter were opposed on the grounds that it was neither feasible nor necessary.

By 1976 the Schools' Council was sufficiently confident of the desirability of a joint 16-plus examination to recommend it to the Secretary of State. The Minister, however, considered that an independent study was needed. Accordingly, in 1977, the Waddell Committee was appointed with a remit to oversee that study. In 1978 the Committee reported that a single system of examining at 16-plus was both desirable and feasible (Waddell Report, 1978). The Committee recommended: the use of a seven-point grading scale correlated with existing GCE/CSE standards; the establishment of consortia of existing GCE and CSE examination boards; the creation of a central co-ordinating body to seek national agreement on criteria for subject titles, syllabuses and assessment procedures; and the introduction of papers designed for the extremes of the ability range. The new target date for the examination was set for 1985.

A Government White paper in 1978 endorsed the regional examination authorities and the central co-ordinating body and mentioned the drawing up of national criteria, but set no target date for the new examination (Department of Education and Science, 1978). However, the change of government in 1979 led to delays.

The new administration, whilst accepting the principle of a common 16-plus, did not accept all the proposals in the White paper. (For example, the new Government wanted the examination to be based on the standard of 'O' level.) But in February 1980 the Secretary of State announced the Government's intention of introducing a new system of examinations at 16-plus (Department of Educational Science, 1980a). The Government stressed that it was not merely introducing a new single examination for pupils covered by GCE/CSE (60 per cent of the ability range) but a new system, with the possibility of there being alternative papers of varying difficulty for different ability groups. Whereas the previous Government's proposals were for the eight GCE and the fourteen CSE boards to merge into five regional groups (each including at least one GCE board) under the new plans the boards, initially at least, would retain their separate identities within the new groups.

The Secretary of State requested that national criteria for the new system be drawn up so that syllabuses with the same title had similar content and so that all boards applied the same performance standards to the awards of grades. It was proposed that the GCE boards be allowed the right to control the three highest grades of the examination. Joint GCE/CSE working parties for each subject were asked to develop the national criteria and to describe the expected attainment of candidates in grade 3 and grade 6 of the proposed seven-grade system, in an attempt to make grading criteria explicit and for these to be based on attainment rather than statistical norms.

Progress towards the introduction of the joint 16-plus has proved to be a protracted and tendentious affair. Criticisms have been levelled at the proposed board structure; at the potential divisiveness of the examination; at the grading system; and at the draft national criteria. The independence of the boards within their consortia has been criticized as being potentially divisive and, if they are permitted also to continue to offer the old style examinations, potentially sabotaging (Macintosh, 1982; Price, 1981). The danger of segregation was reinforced by the frequent references made to the different functions of the two sets of boards (GCE/CSE) in relation to different grades within the new grading scheme. For the new 16-plus to be unified an integrated administrative structure would seem to be an essential prerequisite, yet the existence of two kinds of boards would seem to militate against unity.

The grading system of papers and marks to be used in assessing performance has also been fraught with difficulties and unanswered questions. Should there be a single examination or a single system? Should there be questions or papers of varying difficulty to test pupils across the full ability range? If so, should there be a choice between them so that candidates can opt for a harder or an easier route? How could the grades awarded allow for a mediocre performance on a 'hard' question or paper compared to a good performance on an 'easy' question or paper? Although the move towards a new system ostensibly is intended to overcome many of the difficulties of the current GCE/CSE, in practice some candidates could be worse off if there were no way in which they could obtain the higher grades. A Schools' Council report which examined three possible techniques (common examinations; common papers plus an equal option; and differentiated examinations) appears to favour differentiated examinations whilst recognizing the statistical problems of equating marks with grades (Tattersall, 1983).

When the Secretary of State asked for acceptable draft national criteria to be drawn up, prior to Government approval of a joint 16-plus, no indication was given as to what the criteria could or should be (Macintosh, 1982). The criteria which have been put forward have been the subject of considerable criticism and, in some cases, rejection by both teacher and subject associations or by the Secretary of State (O'Connor, 1982; Doe, 1982). For example the Secretary of State, who at times appeared equivocal over the introduction of a new examination, expressed dissatisfaction with proposed draft criteria for physics. These were submitted by the Joint Council for 16-plus National Criteria, in conjunction with teachers, the Association for Science Education (ASE), The Institute of Physics, the CBI and H.M. Inspectorate — all of whom argued that science syllabuses should emphasize the wider social and economic implication of the subject. The criteria were turned down by Sir Keith Joseph on the grounds that they might make the teaching of science 'tendentious' (*The Times Educational Supplement,* 1983, 18 March and 15 April). The ASE and the NUT, in turn, rejected the rejection (*The Times Educational Supplement,* 1983, 20 May).

In April 1982, the Secretary of State announced that the Schools Council was to be abolished and replaced by two Government-appointed bodies: the Secondary Examinations Council, to co-ordinate and supervise the conduct of examinations at 16-plus and 18-plus, and the School Curriculum Development Committee which would play an advisory role in relation to the curriculum.

Sir Keith Joseph's Sheffield Speech (January 1984)

On 6 January 1984, Sir Keith Joseph proposed a number of reforms to raise school standards and pupils' achievements in a speech at the North of England Education Conference in Sheffield. Much of the speech was concerned with the quality of teaching and the need for an agreed curriculum from 5 to 16. The principal thrust, however, was directed towards examinations. In particular the Secretary of State argued against the use of norm-referencing in 16-plus examinations:

> . . . we should move towards a greater degree of criterion-referencing in these examinations and away from norm-referencing. The existing system tells us a great deal about relative standards between different candidates. It tells us much less about absolute standards. We lack clear definitions of the level of knowledge and performance expected from candidates for the award of particular grades . . . We need a reasonable assurance that pupils obtaining a particular grade will know certain things and possess certain skills or have achieved a certain competence.

On 20 January members of the House of Commons debated the implications of the Secretary of State's speech. Examinations were discussed by
a number of M.Ps. Support for Sir Keith Joseph's initiative came from
all major political parties, although members on all sides emphasized the
resource implications inherent in the speech.

Thus, John Cartwright (SDP/Liberal Alliance) welcomed the Secretary
of State's recognition both of the need to increase motivation and achievement across the entire ability range and of the potential benefits of moving
towards a system which assessed absolute, rather than relative, standards.
However, Cartwright was sceptical whether Sir Keith's objectives could
be achieved 'against the background of massive expenditure cuts' and
'disastrous' rate-capping. (*Hansard* 20 January 1984, p.291, Col. 556).
Harry Greenway (Conservative) 'warmly welcomed' the move towards a
criterion-based system of assessment: 'It could be applied to the development of regular graded assessments, and that is one of its great strengths'
(Ibid., p.294, Col. 562). Greenway concluded, however, that 'it is
unrealistic to think that standards can be raised without resources'. Support from the Labour benches came from the Opposition Spokesman, Giles
Radice. He recognized that 'the pressure of examinations on secondary
schools at present often limits and narrows the curriculum, to the detri-
ment of pupils at all levels of ability. *Examinations should be the servant,
not the master'*. (Ibid. p.309, Col. 591, our italic). Radice welcomed the
part which criterion-referenced examinations could play in an assessment
system which fostered self-confidence and achievement, but he considered
that 'an effective national profile system of records of achievement for
all pupils' was also needed. The Secretary of State was pressed, by the
Opposition Spokesman, to take a decision on the future of the 16-plus
examination.

In reply, Sir Keith Joseph stated that a decision would be taken 'in the
second quarter of this year' (Ibid., p.314, Col.601) on whether to establish
a single system of grades or to harmonize separate 'O' level and CSE
grades.

General Certificate of Secondary Education (GCSE)
In the event, the long-awaited announcement was made by the Secretary
of State in the House of Commons on 20 June 1984. It had been decided
that pupils would begin studying for the new examination, to be known
as the General Certificate of Secondary Education (GCSE), in the autumn
of 1986 and that the first papers would be taken in the summer of 1988.

Broadly speaking, the new examination system would have *five* main features. It would be administered by five groups of GCE and CSE boards, four in England and one in Wales, and be monitored by the Secondary Examinations Council. All syllabuses and assessment and grading procedures would follow nationally agreed guidelines, known as the 'national criteria'. Furthermore, these 'national criteria' would be extended as soon as practicable to embrace a new and more objective system of 'criteria-related' grading in which the grades awarded to candidates would depend on the extent to which they had demonstrated particular levels of attainment defined in 'grade criteria'. (It has to be admitted that many observers regard this as being both philosophically undesirable and practically impossible.) The 'national criteria' would make provision for differentiated assessment, by means of differentiated papers or differentiated questions *within* common papers, in each subject, and for relating coursework tasks to candidates' individual abilities. Finally, GCSE grades would be awarded on a single, 7-point scale (as shown in Table 4), the GCE boards bearing special responsibility within the groups for maintaining the standards of grades A to C, and the CSE boards bearing a similar responsibility for grades D to G (Department of Education and Science, 1985).

Table 4: Grading scale for the new GCSE

O-level	GCSE	CSE
A	A	
B	B	1
C	C	
D	D	2
E	E	3
	F	4
	G	5

Criticisms

The introduction of this new examination has been surrounded by a good deal of controversy. Much of this has concentrated on the related issues of finance and resources. An article in the *Guardian* in April 1986 called GCSE the 'General Certificate of *Skinflint* Education' and pointed out that at that time all that was promised by the Government was £20 million over two years for books and equipment — a sum which, when filtered down to the schools, amounted to about £25 per pupil (O'Connor, 1986). The National Association of Head Teachers suggested that £100 per pupil would be more realistic, with an extra grant of £5,000 per school for the purchase of major items of equipment. Moreover, delegates to the Confederation of Parent-Teacher Associations meeting in York in April 1986 voted unanimously to call for a postponement of the GCSE launching date unless the Government made immediately available sufficient resources for text books and equipment — estimated to be around £100 million — and adequate time for in-service training (*Observer*, 1986, 6 April).

For a long time, the three largest teachers' unions (the NUT, NAS/UWT and AMMA), many local authorities and two out of five of the new GCSE Examining Boards were opposed to the introduction of the new courses in September 1986. It was argued that a number of schools had not received the national criteria and draft syllabuses, that large numbers of teachers had not yet been trained to teach the courses, and, most important of all, that schools and colleges were being expected to embark on a radical new experiment from a base which had been seriously depressed over a number of years. Yet Sir Keith Joseph and his ministers were not prepared to countenance any sort of delay; and the new examination will go ahead supported by the provision of a further £20 million announced in June 1986 by the new Secretary of State, Kenneth Baker.

At the same time the GCSE has not been without its critics who have voiced objections on philosophical grounds. As we have seen, early criticisms were levelled at the potential divisiveness of the joint 16-plus, with the danger of segregation being reinforced by the different functions of the two sets of boards (GCE/CSE) within the proposed new system. In 1982, Nuttall argued that the original proposals of the Schools Council and of the Waddell Committee had been watered down to such an extent that 'they began to look more like a common grading scheme for two examinations, rather than a common system of examining'. His analysis was sufficient to convince him, that the promise of a comprehensive and liberating examination system to match a comprehensive education system has been lost, and that the system we are likely to get, after years of stultifying bureaucratic and political manoeuvering within the DES, is divisive, retrogressive, incapable of developing, obsolescent in that it is not likely to meet today's curricular needs, let alone tomorrow's, and anti-educational, in that it will not be sensitive to the needs of pupils, teachers, classrooms, schools and even society itself (Nuttall, 1982).

Nuttall's observations would still appear to be relevant four years later.

Administratively, there are a number of changes which have been generally welcomed: simpler entry procedures, a common timetable of papers nationally and a shorter examination season. But these would appear to amount to little more than a tidying-up operation. It would, in the view of many critics, be wrong to see GCSE as a truly radical initiative. *The Times Educational Supplement* has argued (29 November 1985) that the new examination marks the triumph of a subject-dominated curriculum:

It is now clear that all the Inspectorate's efforts to steer curriculum planning towards an exploration of a full range of areas of experience have failed to lift the secondary school programme out of its entrenched subject-defined tradition. By the time the SEC (Secondary Examinations Council) has done its best (or worst), any notion of a core curriculum will have to be found in the form of a spread of GCSE entries.

It has also been pointed out, in an article in the *Guardian,* that the new system does not even solve the problem of having more than one examination to choose from.

Many months before the examination, pupils will be segregated into those who will answer the hard papers and questions and those who will answer the easy ones. To reinforce this, the GCE boards will be responsible for the standard of the top grades and the CSE boards for the bottom grades. This is little different from the GCE/CSE dual system except that the segregation will be hidden, all certificates being headed GCSE (Mathew, 1986).

Moreover, the element of coursework provided for in the subject-specific criteria may not always prove to be particularly significant. It could be argued that the CSE Mode 3 option afforded far more scope for meaningful school-based curriculum development.

Target group

As we have seen, the GCE/CSE structure was designed for the top 60 per cent of the relevant age-group leaving 40 per cent of children outside the system. In practice, around 90 per cent of youngsters were brought within the orbit of the GCE/CSE examination — even if many pupils were attempting only one subject at CSE level. The target group for the new GCSE examination is less clearly defined. In the words of the DES introductory booklet:

> The standards required of successful candidates in GCSE examinations will be not less exacting, grade for grade, than those required in the existing O-level and CSE examinations . . . [GCSE examinations] will be designed, not for any particular proportion of the ability range, but for all candidates, whatever their ability relative to other candidates, who are able to reach the standards required for the award of particular grades in each subject . . . The Government seeks . . . a progressive raising of standards of attainment. As and when this happens, the proportion of pupils obtaining graded results will naturally be greater in the GCSE than in the existing examinations (Department of Education and Science, 1985, p.3).

Still no common system

Yet, despite these good intentions, it seems clear that the new examining structure for years four and five will not be a unified one. Already there are signs that FE examining bodies will be allowed to peddle their wares alongside GCSE to compete for the custom of 15 to 16-year-olds. The Joint Board for Pre-Vocational Education issued a press release in January 1984 to announce that:

> BTEC and CGLI see their decision to adopt a joint approach to pre-vocational education as a major contribution to helping schools and colleges provide young people with a more effective transition from school to work. The two bodies want to create a new curriculum pathway for that majority of those between the ages of 14 and 18 for whom the traditional academic curriculum is unsuitable.

This was followed by a further statement in September 1985 announcing that:

> the Councils of BTEC and City and Guilds have agreed jointly to develop and operate a new pre-vocational provision for students aged 14-16 which will offer a national alternative to traditional subject-based school courses.

So much for a common system of assessment at 16-plus.

Conclusion

Paradoxically, many of us who have supported, for a number of years, the idea of a common examination have now moved beyond that idea in our thinking. To create solely a unified examination for 16-year-olds — even one based on clear criteria — could be criticized for being counter-productive. Having waited so long for reform, it seems to us that the time has now passed when the contribution to education of a joint 16-plus would have been greatest. The focus on getting the new examination right, and the statistical difficulties of providing one examination for the whole age group, could detract from what many see as the exciting, flexible and co-operative approach inherent in a system of criterion-referenced graded assessments. Current draft criteria tend to favour techniques that are convenient for large-scale administration — the conventional written paper — and frown upon school-based assessment. But, as Nuttall has pointed out (1982), 'criteria *could* be written that liberate assessment and ensure that wider educational aims are fostered'. We have, of course, to accept that the GCSE examination has arrived and will be with us for a number of years. With this in mind, our final chapter 'The Way Forward' looks at ways in which new and progressive approaches can be incorporated within the GCSE framework.

6 The Way Forward

Formal written examinations were first introduced into British education at the beginning of the nineteenth century. They were used initially in universities (for admission and graduation) and to control entry to the professions. Their use in schools has been characterized by an ambivalence over whether, principally, they were a measure of the school and teachers (as in the original 'Locals' and the payment by results system) or of the individual pupils (matriculation, 'O' levels, 'A' levels, etc.). From the earliest forms of examinations there has also been a clear split between 'academic' examinations such as the School Certificate and GCE papers and the 'less-academic' examinations such as City and Guilds, RSA, CSE, CEE and the new CPVE.

There has also been a failure to consider the examination system as a whole. Each of the various proposals for reform ('Q' and 'F', 'N' and 'F', 'I' level, the CEE, and the new GCSE) have concentrated on a single age group. Most proposals have in the end been rejected, in particular by the universities which, through the examination boards, have maintained control of the 'academic' examinations. The rationale for rejection has usually been the need to protect the standard of university entrants.

It is apparent that the English and Welsh systems incorporate many more examinations than do the systems of most other countries. Whilst other countries, such as France and the United States, admit students to universities on the basis of performance in examinations, their systems are rather different to that of England and Wales. In the case of France, once students have passed the *Baccalauréat* they have a right to a university place. In our system students with the necessary 'A' level qualifications still have to compete for a limited number of places. The American system, unlike that of England or France, provides competitive examinations only for those intending to enter university. Those not intending to do so can successfully complete their education and gain a high school diploma without sitting for these examinations. Other industrialized countries such as Sweden rely on a combination of teacher-assessment, graded assessments or individual pupil profiles. These successful industrialized societies have found ways of assessing pupils' learning that do not involve formal public examinations.

In this final section four key questions are posed. They are:

(i) Do the disadvantages outweigh the advantages of the current examination system?

(ii) Do we have the means to design and develop alternative forms of assessment?

(iii) Will the proposed changes be a 'panacea' for the problems besetting secondary schools?

(iv) How can change be implemented?

(i) Do the disadvantages outweigh the advantages of the current examination system?
Without doubt there are advantages to an externaly validated examination system. It can provide benchmarks of achievement and can deliver credentials to employers and selectors; it serves to motivate pupils and teachers; it provides feedback on the attainment of educational objectives; it rewards merit; it is objective; and, to some extent, its existence has increased opportunities.

These are advantages, however, which at best apply to that 60 per cent of the secondary school population for whom the GCE and CSE were designed. At worst they apply only to the 15 to 20 per cent of the age group who achieve the 5 'O' level equivalents that many employers (and some teachers and parents) regard as the badge of success. Yet the limitations imposed on the curriculum by examinations affect all pupils whatever their ability. Moreover, the methods of the examination boards lead to the difficulties of a norm-related system which as we have argued (see page 27) result in approximately the same proportion of candidates being awarded a similar number of grades each year, whatever their performance. Added to this are the statistical problems of comparability between different examination boards. The reliability of results is increasingly recognized as being approximate rather than precise — yet it is seen by many pupils, teachers and parents as being a true reflection of either attainment or ability. Finally, and most disturbing of all, the system may not serve well even the brightest pupils. Because it is so heavily reliant on timed, written answers, there is a tendency to encourage the skills of rote learning and the reproduction of facts rather than the testing of judgement and problem solving. It seems clear to us, therefore, that the disadvantages of the present system do outweigh its advantages. Although the new GCSE will attempt to move away from norm referencing (see p.71 above) it has yet to be seen whether it will overcome this balance of disadvantage.

The current system of assessment is so fraught with difficulty, so limiting in its effects on teaching and learning, and so likely to damage the self-esteem of so many (possibly the majority), that it cannot be in the best interests of our society. If there are any other means by which the advantages of examinations noted above could be retained (that is, providing the necessary assessment, feedback and motivation for all pupils without endangering standards) these surely should be given serious consideration.

(ii) Do we have the means to design alternative forms of assessment?
Moves towards devising alternative forms of assessment are already under way. In this paper we have described two of these: profiles and graded assessments. As yet development of these alternatives is at an early stage. As we have noted, considerable technical problems have to be overcome. Yet the opportunity to adopt a more encompassing system, building on what the majority of pupils can do rather than pinpointing what they cannot, does exist.

Profiles, offering a broad, longer-term picture of a pupils' development, with a component contributed by the pupil, are capable of providing considerably more information to all interested parties than can a GCE or CSE certificate. A wide range of skills and achievements for all pupils can be recognized and rewarded.

Graded assessments present different opportunities. They can be progressive, offer short-term goals and they do not depend necessarily on statistical norms. These characteristics are of great significance when they are compared to the drawbacks of the current system where public examinations are not progressive but are taken by most pupils immediately prior to leaving school.

Could these two methods of assessment be related to each other and, if so, could they then meet the necessary criteria of the provision of benchmarks, feedback, motivation, etc.? We believe they could, provided essential technical work on development is accomplished. The notion of linking profiles and graded assessments (despite their differing origins in qualitative and quantitative methodologies) has already been adopted by some local authorities and examining bodies. For example, the ILEA has been developing a London Record of Achievement (Inner London Education Authority, 1982). This will consist of a portfolio containing the results of graded assessments and other examinations, and a profile compiled by teachers, parents and pupils. Similar to the London portfolio is the Oxford Certificate of Educational Achievement currently being devised by the Oxford Delegacy of Local Examinations and the Oxford University Department of Educational Studies, in collaboration with a number of local authorities (O'Connor, 1983).

We believe that, given adequate development work, profiles and graded assessments could provide more benchmarks than do current conventional examinations which are taken only at the end of the fifth year — usually on hot June afternoons at the height of the hay fever season! They could also provide credentials for employers and selectors for training or further or higher education. They would, in fact, be capable of providing more detailed information on a pupil's achievements and abilities, since all the eggs would not be in a one-off examination basket. The shorter-term objectives, regular feedback, opportunities for pupil participation, and the chance for more pupils to succeed could enhance pupil and teacher motivation. A broader concept of ability — one which embraced a range of personal skills and which permitted more diverse application of knowledge — could be rewarded. This, in turn, could increase the opportunities for some success for a greater proportion of pupils. In addition, new methods of assessment also would provide the opportunity for much of the curriculum development currently limited by the constraints of the examination system.

The introduction of a new system could provide the opportunity to reduce the inevitablity of failure. Graded assessments could allow many more pupils to achieve some success and to be spared the scarring effects of failure that so inhibit motivation or further study. The avoidance of unnecessary failure may, in turn, trigger the potential for success in a higher proportion of pupils than at present. Assessment would then play its proper part in the educational process by *facilitating* rather than *inhibiting* effective learning.

What is needed now is the development back-up to answer some of the statistical problems of profiles and graded assessments, so that any new system does not falter on inadequate foundations or spurious assumptions.

(iii) Will the proposed changes be a 'panacea' for the problems besetting secondary schools?

Any changes to the systems of assessment of secondary pupils are unlikely, by themselves, to solve all the problems of secondary education. Even if statistical problems of validity and reliability are resolved adequately, the underlying issue of social selection will remain. In the current system, public examinations have a clear social selection function. Pupils, in general, leave school with a sense of acceptance of their future place in society. To a certain extent compulsory education has taken over the function of providing differential access to power, money and status that class and privilege previously operated. (Happily there are exceptional individuals whose social mobility does not conform to the overall patterns.)

Unfortunately, selection operates by legitimating school failure. Thus an efficient system of social selection depends on the acceptance of failure by a majority of school pupils. Any change which would result in fewer pupils considering themselves failures would, surely, be beneficial. The problems of social selection would, however, be increased. If schools were no longer efficient sorting devices, then undoubtedly other mechanisms would develop to take over this function. Thus, for example, universities might set their own entry examinations and industry and business might establish more searching selection procedures. The question must, therefore, be asked as to whether, by transferring selection functions from school to post-school, anything worthwhile would be achieved.

We believe that three advantages could accrue from such a move. First, the logic accepted in the principle of comprehensive education would be furthered by the transfer of social selection (already transferred from the age of eleven to sixteen) to the post-school stage. Second, the advantages for schools in no longer being a part of the process of failure, could be considerable and, as a result, much of the painful conflict that is currently manifest between failing pupils and their teachers might be reduced. Third, we believe that by removing the mechanisms of social selection to an older age group, the influence of background factors (family, class, gender and ethnicity) might be reduced. The older those being selected, the more likely it is that individual talents, motivation, skills and achievements would be considered, and that these would reflect the striving of the individual rather than their background.

These three advantages, in our opinion, justify change. They will not, however, provide a panacea for all difficulties. For example, the problem, elegantly expounded by Hargreaves, of how suitable is the standard secondary curriculum, remains to be solved in other ways (Hargreaves, 1982).

What is important, however, is that by reviewing the methods of assessment and by introducing means of recording achievement which are free from the problems of the current system, the opportunity exists to raise standards.

(iv) How can change be implemented?

The extent to which previous attempts at reform of the examination system have led to opposition and prevarication has been described in Chapter 5. This opposition and prevarication undoubtedly reflects deep-seated resistance to change. Unless such resistance can be overcome, little progress is likely to be made in developing more positive techniques of assessment.

Despite our reservations, we nonetheless feel that real advance can be made *within* the proposed new GCSE framework. There are ways in which the new structure can incorporate flexible and progressive features. The courses taken by pupils can be broken down into units, thereby utilizing a modular approach (as recommended in the Hargreaves Report *Improving Secondary Schools,* 1984); the expertise of those working with graded assessments can be capitalized upon to provide assessments at key points; and achievement can be recorded and stored in the profiles of the pupils, which will then provide a continuous record of their progress through secondary school. At appropriate points, the 'interim' records of achievement can be 'cashed-in' for externally-produced Statements of Achievement which will primarily serve a summative function. The whole scheme, including the award of 'interim' documents, can be monitored by external moderators in partnership with the schools.

Educational reforms have come a long way in just over one hundred years of state education, but the divisive nature of the system is still apparent. Reforms have failed, so far, to achieve expected levels of social justice. As a society we surely cannot afford to imbue so many young people with a sense of educational failure. The challenge to educators to achieve a just system of assessment is clear. To respond to the challenge half-heartedly would be short sighted; to ignore it could be disastrous.

* * * *

List of References

Balogh, J. (1982), *Profile Reports for School Leavers*. Longman/Schools Council.

Beloe Report (Secondary Schools Examinations Council, 1960), *Secondary School Examinations other than the GCE*. HMSO.

Benn, C. (1980), 'Selection still blocks growth of Comprehensives', *Where?* 158, May. Advisory Centre for Education.

Binyon, M. (1970), *The Times Educational Supplement,* 19 June, 26 June and 3 July.

Boucher, L. (1982), *Tradition and Change in Swedish Education*. Pergamon.

Broadfoot, P. (1979), *Assessment, Schools and Society*. Methuen.

_____ (1980), 'How exams cheat our children', *New Society,* 19 June.

_____ (1982), 'Alternatives to public examinations', *Educational Analysis,* Vol.4 No.3.

_____ (1982a), 'The pros and cons of profiles', *Forum,* Vol.24, No.3, Summer.

Brophy, J. and Good, T. (1974), *Teacher/Student Relationships: Causes and Consequences*. Holt, Rinehart and Winston.

Browne, S. (1983), reported in *The Times Educational Supplement,* 1 April.

Bryce Report (1895), *Report of the Commission on Secondary Education*.

Burgess, T. and Adams, E. (1980), *Outcomes of Education*. Macmillan.

Burstall, C. and Kay, B. (1978), *Assessment: The American experience*. HMSO.

Cambridge University Local Examinations Syndicate (1976), *Examinations at 16-plus: Summary of the Syndicate's Comments on the Report to the Schools Council,* February.

Central Advisory Council for Education (England) (1954), *Early Leaving*. HMSO.

Chitty, C. (1980), 'Freedom of choice and the common curriculum', *Forum,* Vol.22, No.3, Summer.

Cockroft Report (1982), *Mathematics Counts,* Department of Education and Science. HMSO.

Consultative Committee on Examinations in Secondary Schools (1911), *Report of the Committee*.

Cookson, C. (1978), *The Times Educational Supplement,* 10 February.

Cooper, F. (1981), 'Graded examinations in science', *Science News,* No.18, June. ILEA.

Corbett, A. (1983), *The Times Educational Supplement,* 24 June.

Crowther Report (Central Advisory Council for Education, 1959), *15 to 18.* HMSO.

David, P. (1983), *The Times Educational Supplement,* 3 June.

Department of Education and Science (1978), *A Single System at 16-plus* (Cmnd 7368). HMSO.

_____ (1979), *Aspects of Secondary Education: A survey by H.M. Inspectors of Schools.* HMSO.

_____ (1980), *Examinations 16 to 18: A consultative paper.* HMSO.

_____ (1980a), press release, 19 February.

_____ (1981), press release, 3 April.

_____ (1982), *17-plus: A new qualification.*

_____ *(1985), General Certificate of Secondary Education; A general introduction.* HMSO.

Department of Employment (1986), *Working Together: Education and Training* (Cmnd 9823). HMSO.

Dockrell, W. and Black, H. (1978), *Assessment in the Affective Domain: What can be done about it?* Scottish Council for Research in Education.

Doe, B. (1981), 'For low achievers only', *The Times Educational Supplement,* 3 April.

_____ (1982) *The Times Educational Supplement,* 8 January.

Duckworth, D. (1975), *The Experimental Certificate of Extended Education.* Schools Council/NFER.

Duffy, M. (1980), 'A log book of personal achievement', *Education,* 1 February.

Dundas-Grant, V. (1982), *Comparative Education,* Vol.18, No.1.

Education (1983), 4 February.

Entwistle, N. and Wilson, J. (1977), *Degrees of Excellence.* Hodder and Stoughton.

Fagg, M. (1983), *The Times Educational Supplement.* 7 October.

Fletcher, C. (1980), 'The Sutton Centre profile', in Burgess and Adams op cit.

Floud, J., Halsey, A. and Martin, F. (1956), *Social Class and Educational Opportunity.* Heinemann.

Forbes, R. (1982), 'Testing in the USA', *Educational Analysis,* Vol.4, No.3.

Forrest, G. (1972), *Standards in Subjects at the Ordinary level of the GCE, June 1970,* Joint Matriculation Board.

Foster, G. (1983), 'Examining at 17-plus', *Secondary Education,* Vol.13, No.1, March.

Further Education Unit (1979), *A Basis for Choice: Report of a study group on post-16 pre-employment courses.*

―――― (1981), *Vocational preparation.*

―――― (1982), *Profiles.*

――――(1984), *Profiles in Action.*

―――― *(1985), CPVE in Action: The Evaluation of the 1984/85 Pilot Schemes.*

Geddes, D. (1982), 'Second thoughts on exams', *The Times,* 11 February.

Gipps, C., Steadman, S., Blackstone, T. and Stierer, B. (1983), *Testing children: Standardized testing in local education authorities and schools.* Heinemann.

Goacher, B. (1982), 'Records of achievement', *Newsletter 1,* Schools Council.

―――― (1983), *Recording Achievement at 16-plus.* Longman/Schools Council.

Goldstein, H. (1982), 'Models for equating test scores and for studying the comparability of public examination', *Educational Analysis,* Vol.4, No.3.

Gray, G., Rutter, M. and Smith, A. in L. Hersov and I. Berg (1980), *Out of School: Modern perspectives in truancy and school refusal.* John Wiley.

H.M. Inspectorate (1983), *A Survey of the Use of Graded Tests of Defined Objectives and their Effect on the Teaching and Learning of Modern Languages in the County of Oxfordshire.* Department of Education and Science.

Hadow Report (Consultative Committee to the Board of Education, 1926), *The Education of the Adolescent.* HMSO.

Harding, A., Page, B. and Rowell, S. (1980), *Graded Objectives in Modern Languages.* Centre for Information on Language Teaching.

Hargreaves, D. (1967), *Social Relations in a Secondary School.* Routledge and Kegan Paul.

―――― (1982), *The Challenge for the Comprehensive School: Culture, curriculum and community.* Routledge and Kegan Paul.

Harrison, A. (1982), *Review of Graded Tests,* Examinations Bulletin 41. Schools Council.

Hedger, J. (1982), 'A new pre-vocational qualification', *Coombe Lodge Report,* Vol.15, No.9.

Holmes, E. (1911), *What Is and What Might Be.* Constable and Company.

Houts, P. (ed.) (1977), *The Myth of Measurability.* Holt, Rinehart and Winston.

Inner London Education Authority (1982), 'Secondary education: further developments', ILEA 2524, Report to Schools Sub-committee.

———— (1984) *Improving Secondary Schools* (Hargreaves Report).

Jackson, M. (1982), *The Times Educational Supplement* 17 December.

———— (1982a), 'New profiling draws heavy criticism' *The Times Educational Supplement,* 19 February.

Jennings, A. (1970), *The Times Educational Supplement,* 3 July.

Joint Matriculation Board (1983), *Problems of the GCE Advanced Level Grading Scheme.*

Judge, H. (1974), *Measurement in Education.* BBC Publications.

Keohane Report (1979), *Proposals for a Certificate of Extended Education,* Department of Education and Science. HMSO.

Labour Party (1982), *16-19: Learning for Life.* Labour Party Discussion Document.

Lacey, C. (1970), *Hightown Grammar: The school as a social system.* Manchester University Press.

———— (1974), 'De-streaming in a "pressured" academic environment' in J. Eggleston (ed.), *Contemporary Research in the Sociology of Education.* Methuen.

Lawson, J. and Silver, H. (1973), *A Social History of Education in England.* Methuen.

Lawton, D. (1980), *The Politics of the School Curriculum,* Routledge and Kegan Paul.

Legrand, L. (1983), *Pour un Collège Democratique la Documentation Francaise.* French Ministry of Education.

Macintosh, H. (1982), 'The prospects for public examinations in England and Wales', *Educational Analysis,* Vol.4, No.3.

Mallinson, V. (1980), *The Western European Idea in Education.* Pergamon.

Mansell, J. (1981), 'Profiling must be a better way', *Education,* 29 May.

———— (1982) 'An FEU Response to 17-plus' *Coombe Lodge Report,* Vol.15, No.9.

———— (1982a), quoted in Broadfoot P., 'The pros and cons of profiles', *Forum,* Vol.24, No.3, Summer.

Marklund, S. (1981), 'Education in a post-compulsory era', *British Journal of Educational Studies,* Vol.29, No.3, October.

Mathews, J. (1986), *Guardian,* 6 May.

Ministry of Education (1955), *Circular 289.*

Mitchell, P. (1982), 'Assessment and record keeping', *Forum,* Vol.24, No.3, Summer.

Mortimore, J. and Blackstone, T. (1982), *Disadvantage and Education.* Heinemann.

National Association of Schoolmasters/Union of Women Teachers (1983), reported in *The Times Educational Supplement,* 13 May.

National Commission on Excellence in Education (1983), *A Nation at Risk.* U.S. Dept. of Education, Washington DC.

——— (1983a), summarized evidence in *Education Week,* 27 April.

National Union of Teachers (NUT) (1970), *The Butler-Briault Proposals: Commentary and Policy Statement,* June.

Neave, G. (1980), 'Developments in Europe' in Burgess and Adams op. cit.

Newcastle Commission (Appointed to Inquire into the State of Popular Education in England, 1861), *Reports of the Assistant Commissioners.*

Newsom Report (Central Advisory Council for Education (England), 1963), *Half Our Future.* HMSO.

Norwood Report (Secondary Schools Examinations Council, 1943), *Curriculum and Examinations in Secondary Schools.* HMSO.

Nuttall, D. (1982), 'Prospects for a common system of examining at 16-plus,' *Forum,* Vol.24, No.3, Summer.

Nuttall, D., Backhouse, J. and Willmott, A. (1974), *Comparability of Standards between Subjects,* Examinations Bulletin 29, Schools Council. Evans/Methuen.

Nuttall, D. and Goldstein, H. (1984), 'Profiles and graded tests: technical issues' in *Profiles in Action.* FEU.

O'Connor, M. (1982), *Guardian,* 23 February.

——— (1983), 'Is this the end of exams as we know them?' *Guardian,* 4 January.

——— (1986), *Guardian,* 29 April.

Orr, L. and Nuttall, D. (1983), 'Determining standards in the proposed single system of examining at 16-plus', *Comparability in Examinations,* Occasional Paper 2. Schools Council.

Oxford and Cambridge Schools Examinations Board (1978), *The 'N' and 'F' Proposals: Comments on the report to the Schools Council,* December.

Oxford Delegacy of Local Examinations and the Southern Regional Examinations Board (1975), *Report to the Schools Council on the 1974 Experimental Examinations in French, History and Physics,* March.

Passmore, B. (1983), *The Times Educational Supplement,* 15 April.

Price, C. (1981), reported in *The Teacher,* 23 October.

Raven, J. (1977), *Education, Values and Society: The objectives of education and the nature and development of competence.* H.K. Lewis.

Rutter, M., Maughan, B., Mortimore, P. and Ouston, J. (1979), *Fifteen Thousand Hours: Secondary schools and their effects on children.* Open Books.

Satterley, D. (1981), *Assessment in Schools.* Basil Blackwell.

Schools Council (1966), *Sixth-form Curriculum and Examinations,* Working Paper 5. HMSO.

_____ (1967), *Some Further Proposals for Sixth-form Work,* Working Paper 16. HMSO.

_____ and Standing Conference on University Entrance (1969), Joint Working Party on Sixth-form Curriculum and Examinations, and the Schools Council Second Sixth-form Working Party, *Proposals for the Curriculum and Examinations in the Sixth Form.*

_____ (1971), *Arguments for a Common System of Examining at 16-plus,* Examinations Bulletin 23. Evans/Methuen.

_____ (1972), *16-19: Growth and Response 1.* Working Paper 45. Evans/Methuen.

_____ (1973), *Review of Comments on Examinations Bulletin 23: 'A common system of examining at 16-plus',* Schools Council Pamphlet 12.

_____ (1973a), *16-19: Growth and Response, 2,* Working Paper 46. Evans/Methuen.

_____ (1973b), *Preparation for Degree Courses,* Working Paper 47. Evans/Methuen.

_____ (1978), *Examinations at 18-plus: Resource implications of an 'N' and 'F' curriculum and examination structure,* Examinations Bulletin 38. Evans/Methuen.

_____ (1979), *Comparability in Examinations,* Occasional Paper 1. Schools Council Forum on Comparability.

_____ (1980), *Examinations at 18-plus: Report on the 'N' and 'F' Debate,* Working Paper 66. Methuen.

Scott-Archer, M. (1982), letter to *The Times Educational Supplement,* 23 February.

Scottish Council for Research in Education (1977), *Pupils in Profile.* Hodder and Stoughton.

Secondary Schools Examinations Council (1947), *First Report.*

Sherwood, P. (1978), 'The testing invasion', *Forum,* Vol.20, No.3, Summer.

Shipman, M. (1980), 'The limits of positive discrimination', in M. Marland (ed.), *Education in the Inner City.* Heinemann.

Smith, L. (1983), *The Times Educational Supplement,* 7 October.

Social Trends 16 (1986). HMSO.

Spens Report (Consultative Committee on Education, 1938), *Secondary Educa-tion, with Special Reference to Grammar Schools and Technical High Schools.* HMSO.

Standing Conference on University Entrance (1979), *The Universities' Views on the 'N' and 'F' Proposals.*

Stansbury, D. (1980), 'The record of personal experience' in Burgess and Adams, op.cit.

Swales, T. (1979), *Record of Personal Achievement: An independent evaluation of the Swindon RPA scheme,* Schools Council Pamphlet 16.

Tattersall, K. (1983), *Differentiated Examinations: A strategy for assessment at 16-plus?* Methuen.

Taunton Commission (Schools Inquiry Commission, 1868), *Report of the Commissioners.*

Tawney, R.H. (1951), *Equality.* George Allen and Unwin.

Waddell Report (1978), *Schools Examinations: Report of the Steering Commit-tee established to consider proposals for replacing the GCE 'O' level and CSE examinations by a common system of examining.* Department of Education and Science.

White, J. (1971), 'The curriculum-mongers: education in reverse' in R. Hooper (ed.), *The Curriculum: Context, design and development.* Oliver and Boyd/Open University Press.

Worby, H. and Bird, M. (1982), 'Record keeping and profiles guidance for schools', ILEA/RS 837/82.